STORIES
BEYOND THE
X's & O's

by

Coach Bob Cortese

with

James E. Alexander, Ph.D.

Foreword by Jeff Rickard

Introduction by Mayor Mick Cornett

ISBN 978-0-9819376-5-6

Published in the USA by

IONIC
PRESS

Design by Hit
www.thehitshow.com

With great appreciation, I dedicate this book to all of my family, friends, players and coaches who have touched my life and made it a wonderful journey.

CONTENTS

FOREWORD

"DO IT AGAIN!" The words of head football Coach Bob Cortese, followed by a short, shrill whistle echoed over the practice field at Mesa State College in Grand Junction, Colorado, at what seemed to be a typical late Thursday practice. It was a cool, crisp autumn evening in the latter part of a Colorado October and as the afternoon sun began its inevitable fall into the horizon, the temperature too, started to wane.

Another whistle was followed by the familiar sound of pads hitting pads, players grunting with great effort and the thunder of forty-four feet attempting to move simultaneously with a purpose. But the coach still didn't like what he was seeing. Another whistle blew and another rendition of "DO IT AGAIN!" rang out across the practice field.

Over and over it was repeated - again and again and again. "DO IT AGAIN!" which was almost always followed by "EVERY PLAYER, EVERY PLAY!" The sun had now fallen completely out of the sky and darkness enveloped the field some 30 minutes after we had collectively attempted what was really just a simple little toss play to the outside. It required a pulling guard, a lead back and a perfect pitch from quarterback Billy Monson to fullback Russ Hodgson. Our starting offense on this top-ranked NAIA team knew what they were supposed to be doing but so too did our scout team defense – and it was a complete stalemate each time they ran it and we stopped it.

With every offensive failure or microscopic mistake – the whistle blew and the words "DO IT AGAIN!" could be heard for miles. After a few minutes of running the play in the semi-darkness, one of the assistant coaches suggested that since visibility was limited, perhaps we should move practice inside for the day. Without hesitation or discussion, Coach Cortese directed everyone to the far west edge of the practice field where there was a small streetlight illuminating perhaps 40 square feet of turf. The misery continued for another 10 minutes in that location until finally, every player performed his job perfectly for what seemed to be three consecutive plays.

Finally, Coach Cortese screamed, "THAT'S GOOD - PERFECT!" and called us in to take a knee, concluding another tough week of practice in preparation for a "typical" conference game.

There would be no great speech at that point. No explanation for the past 40 minutes, nothing to note in any way, that what had just happened wasn't the norm. Nope. There would be nothing but a quick word about tomorrow's walk-through and a reminder concerning what time study hall would commence later that evening.

And that in a quick snap-shot, is my lingering memory of Coach Bob Cortese. As a 20-year-old college football player who was far too small to be playing even NAIA ball, I regarded Bob Cortese as someone bigger than life. He walked and spoke with gruff confidence about everything he was doing and always appeared to have a reason for why he was doing it. At that point in our lives, we were all young men who believed we would be champions simply because Bob Cortese told us it would be so.

Sure, like all young men of that age, we privately questioned his methods and held long off-campus discussions about whether the old man had lost it after a practice such as the one described above – but when he spoke, we listened and when we listened – we won. And we won A LOT. During my two seasons as a part of the Mesa State Mavericks, we accumulated a record of 22-2-2 and our only two losses came in the 1982 and 1983 NAIA national championship games.

In the short span of four seasons, Coach Cortese had turned a perennial bottom-feeder into annual national championship contenders with a core of 17 players he had recruited from Jefferson County on the west side of Denver. He promised his recruits that if they would follow him to Grand Junction and listen to what he preached, they would be conference champions sooner rather than later. The first year that freshmen group (complemented greatly by several other outstanding recruits from out-of-state) went 3-7. The next year they went 7-3. The following two seasons those players would lose only in national championship contests. Coach Cortese had promised success to those players and he delivered in spades.

I had a very unique experience with Coach. I was a late-blooming, scrawny kid who followed my best friend, linebacker John Mark Chisholm, to Mesa State; not only to be with John but also because the school offered a new major in broadcast journalism. I was simply encouraged to go out for the team because I was always in the weight room with John and played ball in the courtyards during my freshman year with other members of the team. Now, when I say scrawny – I'm talking about 5'9" and 145 pounds. I was a natural athlete and could run, throw and catch as well as most of the players on the team – but at my size, I simply couldn't physically compete. So I worked hard at being a kicker and played almost every down in every practice at free safety on the scout team. This was a perfect role for me because there was limited contact and I truly could cover receivers and read plays to the point where I believed I was an asset to the team during the week as I ran the opposing team's defensive coverage schemes. At least Coach Cortese made me feel as if I was an important part of the team.

I never did get to kick in a game since we had one of the most outstanding kickers in the nation on our team, Joe Stellavato, and we were rich in all-conference and all-American defensive backs who were all just a bit bigger than I was. But I showed up for practice and competed every day because Coach Cortese never gave up on me and never stopped yelling at me. Think about that statement. I actually appreciated the fact that Coach Cortese never stopped screaming at me.

That statement makes all the sense in the world because I remember one day during my freshman year (the year before I went out for the team) when as a sports reporter, I was covering practice for the school radio station. I had heard the stories about how hard Coach could be on his players - a real Vince Lombardi type of coach – always yelling, never satisfied and usually making his point with some pretty salty language. He didn't disappoint. While he often spoke normally and rationally, he was just as likely to yell, curse and even grab a player by his shoulder pads to get him into the right position.

On this day, and I will never forget this – he was being hard on our back-up punter about this and that and the other. Over and over he would comment on this young man's abilities with such lines as, "If you don't get better you will have a hard time playing here." Ultimately, the player had enough and actually asked Coach why he was on him all the time. I thought for sure this guy had just purchased himself a one-way ticket off the team or at least off the field. I was surprised when Coach looked the kid right in the eye and said in a very even tone, "Listen – you don't need to worry about how much I yell at you or tell you to do it again; you need to start worrying when I don't say anything to you anymore. Because once I stop talking to you or yelling at you – then it means I've given up on you and don't need to worry about you anymore. Now go back and do it again."

Coach never stopped yelling at me, never stopped coaching me and most importantly, still answered all my questions at the mid-week media days when I took off my football helmet and turned into a reporter asking questions for the team's flagship radio station, KREX. Not only did he coach me on the field – but he treated me with the respect due a real reporter during our radio shows. One time he even sat through an entire "do-over" for a full-length interview that would run during that week's pre-game show after I'd forgotten to turn on the tape recorder at the beginning of the interview.

But I never truly understood how much Coach Cortese cared about me until I was going after a sports anchoring job during my senior year at the local TV station. I was still in school but I had been working for the radio side of the station and thought I would pursue the open anchor job. Mike Nikitas, the news director at the time, was very concerned about this and I was sure I would miss out on the opportunity because of that issue.

About a week later I received a call from Mike offering me the job – with the stipulation that he would be closely monitoring both my work and my school work at the same time. Mike later told me that the biggest reason I got the job was because Coach had taken the initiative to call him personally, on my behalf. Apparently, he had given me a great recommendation. I have never forgotten that or the fact that he never stopped coaching a small, insignificant member of his team each day I showed up to practice. I finally understood that as long as I demonstrated commitment to him, he would always do what he could for me. As long as I was a loyal member of his team, he would always be a loyal member of mine. Besides, as he liked to remind all of us at Mesa State – if we didn't like it there, he would be more than happy to send us off to Ft. Lewis where we could play against him and he'd still "kick our asses." Gotta love the Coach.

And now as I re-read the words I have written above, I have the overriding urge that I always have to contain - the urge to "DO IT AGAIN" until I get it right.

Jeff Rickard

September 2010

Jeff Rickard (also known as "JR") is a sports-talk host on ESPN radio and was formerly the host of "Out of Bounds" for the CN8 cable channel. A graduate of Mesa State College, Jeff was nominated for an Emmy in 2008 and was named the Sports Illustrated Radio Personality of the Year in 2006.

INTRODUCTION

I met Bob Cortese early in 2000. He was the head coach of the Oklahoma Wranglers, an arena football team that had just moved to Oklahoma City from Portland, Oregon. I was the newly installed radio play-by-play announcer. We were both in a transitional point of our lives. Bob, moving into professional football after decades of coaching high school and college players. And me? Well, I was searching for a new start after 20 years of reporting news and sports on television. I really didn't know what my future held but I was anxious to learn more about football and see if I could make a living as a play-by-play broadcaster in the NFL. While I was honing my skills, it didn't take me long to figure out that Bob needed to be a broadcaster as well. His entertaining story-telling style amused me for hours. I was confident that he could do the same on air so we soon launched a radio show called "Strictly Football."

It was a perfect match. I knew enough about football to start the conversation and Bob knew how to explain the details of the sport in a no-nonsense and understandable style. During a commercial break on our first broadcast, Bob started telling me a funny story and I stopped him, "Bob, save your good stuff for when we're on the air." Bob responded in a mock panic, "I don't know what my good stuff is!" Indeed, the best part of the show was when Bob was just talking off the top of his head about one of the many chapters of his coaching life: players he knew, coaches he learned from, jobs he had or jobs he almost got. I learned long ago that many people who like to tell stories about themselves tend to choose the tales that flatter themselves. Bob was different. He told many stories in which he recounted his own mistakes and what he learned from them. In all the stories I've heard from Bob Cortese - and I've probably heard close to 100 - I don't think Bob was the hero in the story more than a dozen times. He was always so honest. And so real. We wound up calling games together. I did the televised play-by-play and Bob played the role of analyst. It was one of the most satisfying segments of my professional life.

Bob frequently noted how much I loved my hometown of Oklahoma City. With his encouragement, I ran for city council and won. He then predicted that someday I would be mayor. I was flattered but it seemed like a pretty far-fetched idea. Alas, our days of working together didn't last. The AFL franchise was dissolved and Bob soon moved away for another coaching job, ending our on-air partnership. Soon after he returned to town, his prediction came true when I did become mayor.

I never played for Bob Cortese but I learned a lot from him. Bob knows people. And if you listen closely to what he says, you will learn a lot about yourself as well.

Mick Cornett
Mayor, Oklahoma City

Mayor Mick Cornett was elected Oklahoma City's 35th mayor in 2004 and is currently serving in his third term. An avid sports fan, Mayor Cornett was an All-State high school athlete before earning his degree in journalism from the University of Oklahoma. He spent 20 years in local television as a sports reporter and anchor. Simultaneously, he worked as a newspaper columnist and sports play-by-play announcer. A visionary leader, Mayor Cornett was elected as a Trustee of the U.S. Conference of Mayors and is the recipient of numerous awards including the "City Livability Outstanding Achievement Award." In recognition of his efforts to use sports as an economic development tool, he was also awarded the Abe Lemons/Paul Hansen Award from Oklahoma City University and the Ray Soldan Media Award from the Oklahoma Basketball Coaches' Association.

Section I

Coaching Years:
Challenges and Championships

1

A General Mistake

– The Wrong Number for the Right Job –

I got my first head coaching job in 1969. It was at St. Joseph High School in Denver, Colorado. St. Joe's, as it was commonly known, was an inner-city parochial school with an enrollment of about 200 students, grades nine through 12. The students tended to be low-income, tough, and mostly minority. Not surprisingly, our football team was pretty salty.

During that year we had a pair of Irish brothers – Kevin Kelly, a senior, and Chris Kelly, a junior. Kevin, who wore number 32, was a very good linebacker. He was tough, had great football instincts, and could always be found around the football. In fact, he was one of the best high school linebackers I ever coached. Kevin's younger brother, Chris, number 23, was a good fullback. Chris started all of our games his junior year and helped us with his aggressive blocking.

After the season ended, I interviewed all the players, one by one, to learn of their future ambitions. Chris was a very good student and always ranked near the top of his class. He told me that he wanted to go to the Air Force Academy after his senior year.

"Coach, after next year I want to attend the Air Force Academy (AFA) and play football," he said.

"You don't need a scholarship to go to the AFA; what you need is a congressional appointment," I told him.

"I know that," he replied. "I have already been working on getting an appointment."

"Keep your grades up and I think there is a real good chance you will get there," I said.

Chris also indicated that during his final year playing high school ball, he would like to wear the number worn by his older brother Kevin during his senior season. Since Kevin would have graduated by then, there was no reason why Chris shouldn't be permitted to wear his sibling's number during his senior year. Hence, Chris Kelly played his senior year as number 32.

When his final football season ended, Chris and I focused on what we could do to get him an appointment to the AFA. We met with his counselor, Sister Diane, to fill out forms, secure recommendations, and submit the application. With the glowing recommendation from one of our state senators, Chris's acceptance would be guaranteed. Or so I thought.

I was wrong. In March, Chris scheduled another appointment with me and Sister Diane. When I saw Chris's demeanor, I knew right away that something was wrong.

"I haven't been accepted to enter the Academy next year," he said lamely.

I was shocked. Chris was a very good student and had all the ingredients needed to be a leader at the military academy. He was honest, hard-working, responsible, reliable, and very intelligent—in short, a perfect fit to be an officer in the United States Air Force.

"I can't believe that you didn't get the appointment!" I said.

Sister Diane, who had remained silent until now, suggested that the problem might be the school's math program. "Chris is an A+ math student here at St Joe's," she said, "but St. Joe's does not have the strenuous curriculum that he needs to compete with students from higher academic high schools. Getting an A+ here isn't good enough for the academies," she said.

"Well, what can we do?" I asked.

"Very little, I'm afraid," the good sister replied. "It's too late now for him to take higher math courses at some other institution."

The disappointment in Chris's eyes was profound. He slumped in his chair, sighing as the enormity of the situation pressed in upon him. Because he attended a poor, inner-city school with low-level math classes, his dream of graduating from the AFA was now apparently squelched.

"I'm going to call Coach Ben Martin," I said. "Maybe he can help circumvent the issue related to the reputation of our math program." Ben Martin was the successful head football coach at the Air Force Academy. I had met him a couple of times over the years at various clinics and football camps. Not only was he a good football coach, but he was also a stand-up guy.

I called Coach Martin. "Chris Kelly is a good football player and a perfect fit for the Academy," I began. I touted Chris as both a good citizen and a good student. I said, "You will enjoy coaching him and I think some day he could develop into someone who can help you win games."

"Bob, we have very strict admission requirements here," he responded. "I will look into his situation but I can't promise that I can help."

Three days later Coach Martin called me back and told me there wasn't anything he could do for Chris. "However," he said, "I can get him into the Air Force prep school where he can continue to work hard and play prep football for a year."

I called Chris and told him what Coach Martin had said. I could tell he was very disappointed and wanted time to think about it. As his coach, I felt bad that Chris was not able to get into the Academy. His disappointment had a strong effect on me.

Later that weekend I ran into Coach Martin at a high school football clinic in Colorado Springs. I tried one more time to see if he could give me any ideas on how Chris might be accepted into the Academy. "Coach, Chris is a perfect fit for you guys," I argued. "He will be a captain for the football team by the time he is a senior."

"How good a player is this kid?" Martin asked.

"He is very good!" I stressed.

"Well, send me some film on him so I can see for myself," he said.

"You bet," I replied.

There was one problem. Since St. Joseph High School did not have much money for its athletic teams, we hadn't actually filmed any games during Chris's senior season. On the other hand, we did have film of a playoff game taken during Chris's junior year and he had played well enough in that game to show off his skills.

As I packed the film, I included a cover note telling all about Chris and his accomplishments as well as his height, weight, and number, forgetting that during his junior year Chris wore number 23 not 32. Thirty-two was the number he wore his senior season, as his brother had the year before.

Chris was a very solid high school player. He would have had an opportunity to help most college football programs. On the other hand, Kevin was a real stud player. Kevin chose not to go to college after high school, but, not surprisingly, was recruited by many schools.

I got a phone call from Coach Martin two days later. "Bob, this kid is pretty good!"

"I told you so," I said confidently.

Martin went on about how aggressive Chris looked on film. He said that since the AFA was looking to recruit a linebacker that year, he thought number 32 would help fill their need. He went on to tell me how impressed he was with the interception and eventual touchdown Chris made to help win the game. He also was very impressed with his effort to block a punt early in the game.

As Coach Martin continued to share the reasons he was impressed with number 32, I gradually came to the embarrassing realization that it wasn't Chris that Martin was raving about—it was Chris's older brother who of course had worn that number the previous year. I just sat there as Coach Martin raved on about how he was going to find a way to get Chris into his program at the Academy.

I soon began to have guilt feelings. I was tempted to call back and tell Coach Martin that there had been a mistake; namely, the player wearing number 32 in that year-old film was actually Chris's older brother, Kevin. That presented me with a dilemma. On the one hand, I had a duty to call Coach Martin and tell him I made a mistake with the listing of numbers I provided. On the other hand, I kept thinking about Chris's disappointment at not getting into the Academy.

I am not proud to say that I put off making that call.

I justified my keeping the secret by convincing myself that Chris would mature into as good a player as his brother had been and would someday help the AFA win football games. In addition, I knew he would make a wonderful officer in the Air Force.

A week later, Chris came running into my office, bursting with excitement. He had finally been accepted to the Air Force Academy! I was happy for him. To this day, I believe that Coach Martin somehow persuaded the admissions office to reconsider Chris, despite the quality of the math program at St. Joe's.

After his sophomore year, Chris decided not to play football anymore. Nevertheless, he remained at the AFA and graduated four years after being accepted.

* * *

Postscript

Following graduation from the Air Force Academy, Chris completed post-graduate programs at the Squadron Officer School, Air Command and Staff College, Industrial College of the Armed Forces as well as a program in National Security Studies. He earned a master's degree in 1984. His Air Force service earned him the following military awards and decorations: Distinguished Service Medal with oak leaf cluster, Defense Service Medal with oak leaf cluster, Legion of Merit with two oak leaf clusters, Bronze Star Medal, Meritorious Service Medal with three oak leaf clusters, and the Air Force Commendation Medal.

In 1993, I received a letter from Chris updating me on his life post-football. He modestly mentioned his many military successes and then closed by saying:

...I can't tell you how many times I think about the old days and how much the things you taught me have meant to me. It is very difficult to put it all into words, but so much of what I am today is the result of having played football for you. Maybe even more important was watching you and how you handled yourself in tough situations. There is no way I can thank you for all of these things. Perhaps the best way is to keep challenging myself and passing on to those who look to me for leadership the things you have taught me...

Chris was wrong about one thing. He said there was no way he could ever thank me – but both his letter and his exemplary life are all the thanks I could ever ask for.

2

The Federal Witness Protection Program
– Handles, Vandals and Algebra –

Your life is not your own when you belong to a gang; the gang owns you.

I learned this important lesson when working with a young man named Jesse Garcia.

Actually, I never knew Garcia's real name. The name "Jesse Garcia" was an alias. Even the alias was an alias—all because he was a former member of, and then a fugitive from, gang-related "justice." I changed his alias to Jesse Garcia because even though these events took place more than a quarter of a century ago, the collective memory of gang members never goes away and their desire for revenge never fades.

I have verified this story with law enforcement officials. They have assured me that by telling the story in the manner I have, that I have protected the identities of the individuals involved.

The story is true. It provides a peek into a very unusual side of athletics. I will piece together information that I did not know at the time, but have learned as the years passed. I still have mixed emotions about participating in this strange and unique situation.

* * *

One hot and sultry summer day, I received a long distance phone call at the state college (name withheld on request) where I was coaching football. The caller was a gentleman who identified himself as a U.S. marshal from another state. He said he wanted to talk with me about a very confidential matter.

The caller told me his name was Jack Henri and stated that he was not at liberty to discuss the situation over the phone. He asked if I would set up a meeting as soon as possible. I said I would. Still, my curiosity was eating away at me as to the hush-hush nature of the *tête-à-tête*, so I slipped in a couple of sneaky questions: "Is this a matter involving one of my players or is this a personal matter?" I asked. Henri very gently reminded me that he wouldn't discuss the matter over the phone. We scheduled an appointment for the following weekend. As we ended our conversation, he again told me not to discuss the meeting with anyone.

"Should I get my lawyer involved?" I asked tentatively.

"No!" he snapped back. "Do not discuss this meeting with anyone! I can assure you that your lawyer will not be needed."

I was concerned at not knowing why a U.S. marshal would want to talk with me. To be perfectly honest, I knew very little about what a U.S. marshal actually did. I was tempted to call my lawyer anyway, or at least seek advice from a couple of friends in law enforcement, but the more I thought about it, the more I decided I'd be better off to cooperate fully with Henri's request for confidentiality.

The following Saturday, I met with Henri and another man, whose name I can't remember. We met in my office. I never did learn why the other guy was at the meeting or what his job was.

The meeting began with Mr. Henri asking questions about the college and its academics. Both men had course catalogs and as Mr. Henri and I talked, the other gentleman browsed through his copy of the catalog. Both men seemed particularly interested in our math program.

After about 20 minutes, Jack Henri finally got to the point. "Coach Cortese, what I am about to share with you must never be discussed with anyone else. I will only give you information that will help you understand what we are trying to do, but not enough information to jeopardize you in any manner." After a long pause, he continued. "We are going to put a Jesse Garcia into the Federal Witness Protection Program. Garcia is not his real name, but that will be what we call him. You don't need to know his real name."

"Okay," I stammered. "What does that have to do with me?"

"He wants to attend college and play football," he responded. "Your school is one we are considering." He went on to explain that it wasn't a good idea for me to know very much about Jesse. "The less you know, the better it will be for him," he said.

"I still don't know why you even need to tell me anything," I said. "Just enroll him in school and have him come out for the team. Why do I have to be told anything?"

Mr. Henri responded, "It is not that easy. We can enroll him in school and have him start taking classes but, periodically, we will need him back in court. He will miss some school and naturally a few of your practices and maybe even a game. We can make up excuses for his missing class time, but it has been our experience that coaches don't tolerate players missing many practices. If he is dropped from the football team or falls from your graces, there is no need for him to be here. Unfortunately, he wants to play football more than he wants to attend school."

Oh good, I thought, *another player who I'll have to put in study tables.*

"Is he going to be a problem for me or my team?" I asked. "I do have a responsibility for the other 100 players."

"I don't think so." Mr. Henri stated. "I think he really wants to turn his life around."

The operative word was "think."

After another 30 minutes discussing dorms, schedules, registration, and tuition, Mr. Henri told me he had another appointment and would get back with me in a week or two. He and his companion, who never said a word, left my office.

Two hours later, I got a phone call from Mr. Henri. He asked me about the potential that Jesse would actually get to play in games. I told him it would depend on his abilities and attitude. He would be given a fair chance to play, but without viewing some film or knowing anything about him, I couldn't possibly answer his question. "If he can help us win football games, he will play. If not, he can practice and learn like everyone else. Let me share with you, however, it will be hard for a freshman to come in here and get a lot of playing time because I have a good team returning." Before the conversation ended, he asked me if I had any players from south Texas or San Antonio in particular. I responded that I did not.

As the call ended, I had the gut feeling that the U.S. marshal and his nonverbal friend had possibly just spent some time on the other side of campus with a member of our administration. I could never confirm it, but it made me feel a little more comfortable thinking that someone, higher up the administrative ladder, was perhaps involved.

I kept my promise not to discuss the meeting with anyone, including my wife. Nothing was set in concrete at the time and I was honestly hoping I wouldn't have to be involved at all.

Two weeks later, I got another call from Mr. Henri. He informed me that Jesse Garcia was enrolling in school and wanted to play football. He inquired about what Jesse needed to do in order to be part of the football team. I told him I needed his address so I could send him all our summer mailings. I then asked, "And how about his phone number so I can at least talk to him before he shows up on my front door?"

"I will have Jesse call you," he said. "He is coming to you from Thunderbird High School in San Antonio, Texas. Remember, he is under a Witness Protection Program so you won't know very much about him or his background." Mr. Henri then gave me his own contact numbers where I could reach him anytime day or night.

"Coach Cortese," I answered as I picked up the phone two days later.

"Hello, Coach Cortese? This is Jesse Garcia," someone responded softly from the other end.

"Hi Jesse, it is good to hear from you," I said. "I heard that you are coming to school here and you want to play some ball."

"Yes, sir," he replied, even more softly than before.

I tried to sound excited and upbeat. "That's good. We are always looking for good ball players to help us win games. What position do you play?"

"I play defensive line," he answered, a little more audibly.

We talked for about 20 minutes. I could tell he had someone helping him respond to a few of my questions. There would be a long pause and then a different sound, like he was putting his hand over the receiver before eventually responding.

Jesse told me he was about 6' tall and weighed around 245 pounds. (Typically, these guys inflate their numbers a bit, which meant that somewhere between 5'10" to 5'11" was probably a more accurate figure.) He played high school football his sophomore year and started the last eight games. His junior year, he was the starter at nose guard and made 74 tackles, five sacks, and six tackles behind the line of scrimmage.

I asked him for his address and told him I would send him a players' letter every week until it was time for him to report to campus. All the information he needed to know would be mailed to him throughout the remainder of the summer. There was a long pause before he provided an address in San Antonio.

I remember the first time I met Jesse. He had just gotten off a bus. His hair was short and black and both arms were covered with tattoos. A gold earring dangled from his left ear as he peered at me through bloodshot eyes. *Uh oh,* I thought, *I hope we don't have a druggie on our hands.* Contrary to my earlier assumptions, however, Jesse appeared to be at least 6' tall with muscles as hard as nails.

During our pre-season practices, Jesse proved that he was a tough guy with a great deal of physical potential. On our third day of practice, for example, we were doing some live one-on-one blocking and tackling drills. On one such drill, Jesse's task was to go up against one of our best senior offensive linemen. As this larger lineman tried to block Jesse, the young freshman struck a vicious blow into his counterpart, tossed him aside, and made a tackle behind the line of scrimmage. Many of the players and coaches got excited to see such a big hit by a young freshman, especially against one of our proven players. When the older player realized that he had just been "taken to the woodshed" by an upstart freshman, he asked to go against him again. Enjoying the moment, I naturally agreed to a second "go-round." Again, the young player defeated his more experienced opponent. This time, after all was said and done, the older and much larger player started a fight with Jesse. Before the coaches could separate the two warriors, Jesse made a move that put the senior flat on his back.

Jesse proved that he belonged on our football team. He was raw in technique, but was aggressive and eager to learn. He worked hard on the field. Even though he hadn't had a great deal of weight training, he was naturally strong and looked like someone we could count on to help win football games.

After the third week of school, we sent out grade check requests to the faculty concerning our players. Jesse's reports were nothing to brag about. Two professors asked to meet with me. First, I met with his English teacher who told me she didn't think Jesse was qualified to be in college. She felt that he lacked writing and reading skills and recommended him for remedial classes. I got a much different story when I met with his math teacher. He said that Jesse was a very special student, and that he wanted to advance him into an elite math program. Apparently Jesse scored in the top 94th percentile on a national freshmen math test. Jesse Garcia was a math wizard.

After the third game of the season, our starting nose guard got hurt and Jesse was moved into the starting lineup. He played well for us. As he got more playing time, his play kept improving. I could tell he was going to be a special player.

On one of our road trips, I had Jesse sit next to me on the bus. We talked for 30 minutes and I felt comfortable that he was enjoying his football experience.

"How are things going for you?" I asked.

"Fine," he replied. "School is hard, but football is banging."

"What about math?" I questioned. "Your math teacher thinks you're special."

"Math comes easy to me," he responded. "I have always found it to be my best subject. Once in high school I won an award for testing out the highest. The other subjects kick my ass." He continued, "You know Coach, I miss my family and friends, but I am sure glad I came here to play football."

I gestured toward his heavily decorated arms and asked, "Do those tattoos have any special meaning?"

"Each one means something," he answered. "For example, the two most important are these," he said, flexing his right bicep to show off a tattoo with the name "Lolita" written in ornate lettering. He turned wistful. "This is my bitch back home. I miss her."

Jesse then pointed to the second tattoo, a fancy one that looked like a double "S." The tattoo was a large letter "S" with a smaller "s" implanted in the middle. "This is my handle," he said. "This is who I am."

Jesse finished the football season as a starter and did help us win most of our remaining games. In one game he blocked a punt that was instrumental in our winning by only three points. He made the all-conference freshmen team and even got some votes as the *Best New Player-of-the-Year* in our league.

After the season ended, I could tell Jesse wasn't as happy as before. I guessed he was homesick and now that he had more time on his hands, he was getting antsy. I kept my eye on him more than I did with most of the other freshmen. I knew he was, for the most part, a fish out of water. Besides football and his math classes, he had nothing here that he considered worthwhile. He was forced to be here because of circumstances.

I got a phone call from Mr. Henri right after Christmas break. "Bob, we are going to relocate Jesse to another part of the country."

"Why?" I questioned. "He's hanging in here and his first semester grades are adequate."

"Things have happened and his being there is not as safe as we once thought," he said in a loud tone. "Don't fuss about this. It is just the way it has to be."

From what I was able to piece together, Jesse had gotten a ride to Salt Lake City to stay with a student friend he met on campus. He planned to spend Christmas vacation with this friend and come back to school for the second semester. Being lonely and missing his girlfriend, Lolita, he invited her to meet him in Salt Lake City for a few days. Not understanding the potential consequences, when the girl returned home, she blabbed where Jesse was located – therefore jeopardizing Jesse's safety.

I never saw Jesse again. He was dropped from school and relocated elsewhere.

* * *

Postscript

A year passed before I found out the rest of the story.

I was in California visiting my brother when he took me to lunch with one of his very good friends. This friend was the head coach at a junior college. During lunch, the coach asked me about a Latino player who he thought had played for me. He didn't know the player's name, but described Jesse quite accurately. I wasn't sure how to respond to his question since I was told not to discuss the matter.

The coach finally told me he knew that I had a player under the Witness Protection Program and that he had recommended my college as a place this player could be safely relocated. The coach continued by telling me he had a brother who was a high school math teacher. One of his students was a math prodigy who was also a member of a very large and dangerous Hispanic gang. This student turned out to be Jesse Garcia. The math teacher and Jesse were close and had a very special relationship.

As a gang member, Jesse was assigned to help kill a rival. He and two other members of his gang were to drive by the rival's home and shoot him. Jesse did not want to follow through with this shooting but, because he was deep in the gang, he had no choice. Either he cooperated with the planned killing or he would be killed himself. It was as simple as that.

The shooting was carried out. Afterwards, Jesse confided to his special friend, the math teacher, that he was in the car as it drove by the rival. Jesse swore that he did not shoot with intent to hit the victim. As the three gang members shot, Jesse made sure he aimed high and was positive none of his bullets hit the victim.

The math teacher convinced Jesse to go to the police and turn state's evidence to convict the other two who were involved in the shooting. Eventually, Jesse became a vital witness in helping the police break up this gang. He told them all about the gang activities and was instrumental in not only solving some crimes his gang had been involved in but also in solving crimes by other gang members outside the state.

The result was that Jesse was now on the hit list for ratting on the members of his former gang. He testified against his former friends and that meant they wanted him dead. The Witness Protection Program was necessary.

Jesse always loved football and since he was a special math student, he and his teacher thought going to college would be best for him. Jesse did not particularly want to go to college but still dreamed of playing football. The math teacher contacted his brother and got a few recommendations of possible colleges to recommend to the U.S. marshals. My school was one of the possibilities and where Jesse initially enrolled.

After Jesse went to Salt Lake City to rendezvous with his girl-friend, he was relocated.

Three years later, my football team won the league championship and eventually lost in the National Playoffs. A week after the season was over, I received the following letter with a Huntsville, Alabama postmark:

Hi Coach,

I saw in the newspaper that you guys had a great season and lost in the playoffs. Sorry you lost but good job anyway. I don't play football anymore but I sure miss it. I was wondering if Joe Little still is playing for you guys. If he is, tell him Jesse said hello. Coach, thank you for helping me and giving me a chance to play ball. It was fun. I just want you to know that I am only 32 hours away from graduating. I can't believe it. I am also planning on getting married next month. I have a daughter and she is 2 years old. Thank you again Coach Cortese and maybe someday I can have you meet my family.

The letter was signed with a large "S" and a smaller "s" inserted in the middle.

3

Recruiting Risks and Rewards

Every football coach has recruiting stories. Some of them are poignant, some are frustrating and some include the fear factor. The following three stories represent some of my experiences and lessons learned in the recruiting realm.

The Value of Relationships
– An Easy No –

I was hired by the University of Colorado as an assistant football coach in January 1978. It was the middle of the month giving me only a couple of weeks before the national signing date of February 14.

My first assignment was to take over recruiting from Dwight Wallace, a handsome young coach who had recently taken the head job at Ball State University. Dwight was a very good recruiter and had an excellent way of warming up to young athletes. He left me a list of very good players he had been recruiting in California.

One of our most pressing needs for the University of Colorado at that time was to recruit a good young quarterback. Since Dwight was also the quarterback coach, he made sure he found and recruit-ed a top prospect. (A good rule for assistant college football coaches is to first and foremost recruit top players who can help win football games. However, they should always, always, make sure they find a good athlete who can play the position that they coach. Good players make coaching much easier. They also make the coach look like he knows what he is doing.)

Bill Mallory, then Colorado's head coach, told me that eventual-ly I would recruit the state of Colorado, but since I was filling Dwight Wallace's vacated position this deep into the recruiting season, he wanted me to follow-up with the players Dwight had been recruiting in California. All the other coaches had been recruiting elsewhere and he didn't think changing them would be the best thing do at this time.

I was hired right out of coaching at Arvada High School, a sub-urb of Denver, and had never done any recruiting before; however, since many of my high school players had been recruited over the years, I knew the characteristics of a good recruiter.

Our staff consisted of George Belu, Floyd Keith, Tom Batta, Gary Durchik, Bob Reubin and Ron Corradini. All these guys were good coaches and recruiters. Whenever I had a question about recruiting, these guys were eager to help.

Since I was hired so near the national signing date, my first task was to get my butt down to California and acquaint myself with the players Coach Wallace had been recruiting. First on my list was a kid named Tim Cowan. Tim was a quarterback who could run and throw the football very well. Coach Wallace had ranked him very high and worked hard to get him to commit to the University of Col-orado. At the time, Coach Jim Mora Sr. was also recruiting Tim for the University of Washington Huskies. Coach Mora later became a very successful head football coach in the NFL. I knew Coach Mora from his earlier days as an assistant at Colorado University. He, like Coach Wallace, was an excellent recruiter.

I flew to California to meet with Tim and his family. With only two weeks to go in the recruiting process, Tim was torn between Colorado and Washington. Tim was scheduled for a recruiting visit to Colorado the last week prior to signing date. That was good for us, because we thought that since we would be his last official visit, we could make the last pitch to get him to sign. Tim had a friend who played for Colorado and that player helped to keep us in touch with what Tim was thinking.

Tim had a great visit in Boulder. Indications were that he really enjoyed himself. When we put him on the plane back to California, he seemed very positive and even told me who he would like to room with his freshman year. I felt confident he would sign.

The following week I flew back to California and started preparing for the opening day of the signing period. I visited with Tim and his relatives the night before signing day to make sure everything was okay and arranged for an early morning visit at his school to officially put ink on paper. I knew Tim's high school coach before I started recruiting Tim. Our paths had crossed at various football clinics throughout the years. I found him to be a good guy and an effective coach.

The next morning, I was raring to go. I wanted to be at the school one minute before signing actually began. With a few extra minutes on my hands, I stopped off at a doughnut shop and bought a bagful of the tasty confections.

When I arrived at Tim's high school, I went directly to the coach's office and asked if he would get Tim out of class so I could sign him as a Colorado Buffalo. I offered the coach the doughnuts; he took one; thanked me and then went to find Tim. When he returned a few minutes later, he had Tim in tow. I could see that Tim did not look very happy. I asked him if he was ready to sign with the Buffaloes. He stared at the floor. *Not good,* I thought. Finally, after what seemed an eternity, Tim sheepishly and softly mumbled that he was not going to sign with Colorado.

I couldn't believe it! After the great visit Tim had to our campus only the week before, the friends already enrolled at Colorado, and the strong visit I had with his family last night, it just didn't seem possible that he had changed his mind. What went wrong? I was dumbfounded. Finally I asked him where he planned to go to school. He answered, "The University of Washington," and then turned and walked out of the office. I looked quizzically at his coach, who simply shrugged his shoulders.

"Do you want your doughnuts back?" he asked. I was so disappointed I almost said yes.

I returned to my rental car and headed out for my next signing appointment. When I got to the freeway, I pulled over to the side of the entrance ramp. I felt I needed to go back to Tim's school and find out what caused him to change his mind and favor Washington. So, with cars beeping their horns at me and drivers showing their displeasure, I backed down the ramp and returned to Tim's school.

Tim's coach was sitting at his desk, sipping a mug of coffee and eating a doughnut. He looked up at me and asked," Did you come back for the doughnuts?"

"No," I said, "I want to talk to Tim again."

The coach shook his head, came around to my side of the desk, and said rather sharply, "Look Bob, Tim made his decision and I don't want you badgering him to change his mind. It's over! Let it go!"

I told him I wasn't there to badger Tim or try to convince him to change his mind. I just needed to find out why he chose Washington over Colorado. "Besides," I said jokingly, "I brought you breakfast this morning."

After it became clear that I wasn't going to put pressure on the kid, the coach reluctantly went and got Tim again. I am sure if this coach hadn't known me, there was no way in hell he would have given me a second chance to talk with Tim. Since I was a recent high school coach in my first college-level recruiting situation, I think he understood my need to know what went awry.

When they came back to the office I wished Tim good luck and asked, "What made you change your mind in such a short period of time?"

Tim stammered and started off by saying how it was a tough decision but did not give me a clear reason why he chose Washington over Colorado. I sighed and said again, "I really need to know why you changed your mind in such a short period of time."

Tim looked me square in the eyes and said, "Coach, I really like Colorado. I love Boulder and the CU campus even more than I like Seattle. I think Coach Mallory is a good coach and I would enjoy playing for him. I also think that I am a better fit for the CU offense than even the Huskies' offense. But, Coach Mora and Coach Wallace both have been recruiting me for more than a year. I have only known you for a couple of weeks and it is a hell of a lot easier for me to tell you I am not enrolling at your school than to face Coach Mora and tell him I won't be going to Washington." He continued, "I think if Coach Wallace was still recruiting me I would have probably come to CU."

Postscript

A short time after Tim signed with the University of Washington, Coach Mora resigned and took a job with the Seattle Seahawks. Tim called me soon after Coach Mora left to see if he could change his decision. We were told he would lose some eligibility, so he never did.

* * *

Promises, Promises

– Six Easy Lessons –

The statute of limitations has long expired on some recruiting rules that were broken back in 1980 at the University of Colorado. Not even the mighty NCAA can roll back the clock and dole out punishment for deeds that occurred so long ago. Moreover, since none of the original participants are still connected with the University, I think I'm safe in telling this story.

At the time, I was an assistant coach at the University of Colorado—in fact, the school's only coach. We were going through a coaching transition. Eddie Crowder, the athletic director, had fired Coach Bill Mallory after the 1979 season. While working to fill the head position, Crowder also fired the entire coaching staff, with one exception. That exception was me. He opted to keep me on as he searched for a new head coach. So, for about two months I was the entire coaching staff at the University of Colorado. I had three graduate assistant coaches helping me keep the program intact until a new head coach was hired.

Recruiting players was always important. But in this case finding good players to work with a new staff, was doubly important. Crowder and I met several times after the mass firings to discuss what the program needed in terms of additional players. Inasmuch as both of our leading rushers had graduated, Crowder and I determined that getting a running back was priority one.

We decided to bring in a junior college running back named Jim Clay, from the Los Angeles area. Clay was a first team junior college All-American running back. He came from a poor family in a poor neighborhood, had gotten married while in junior college, had a car, and owned very little else.

We wanted Clay to enroll in school at mid-semester so that we would have him on campus and ready to go when the new coaching staff took over during spring ball. It wasn't easy to convince him to come and play for us, since so many other schools were recruiting him as well. The fact that I was merely an assistant, in a program without a head coach, made recruiting that much more difficult, indeed, almost impossible as we sought to sign top-drawer talent like Clay.

We did have an ace in the hole, however, a man named Bob Six. He was our number one booster but was better known as the founder and CEO of Continental Air Lines. He and Crowder were good friends. He was also an avid Colorado football supporter and helped the Buffaloes attract national attention. When we told Six that we needed and wanted Clay, he assured us he would do all he could to help recruit him. I am not sure how or what he did to convince Clay to play for the Buffs, but whatever it was, it worked.

I was told that Bob Six invited Jim Clay and his father to have lunch with him aboard his private jet – where he explained the advantages of playing football for the Buffs while they flew over the "City of Angels." He also offered Clay's father a job at the exclusive Country Club Rivera if Clay would play for the Buffs.

Not surprisingly, Jim Clay decided to be a Colorado Buffalo. He and his wife flew to Boulder after being promised – by Six – that his car would be transported from LA. He was also told that arrangements would be made to ship all their belongings to Boulder within two weeks.

Clay and his wife came to Boulder while most students were on semester break. I put them in a hotel until an apartment became available. It snowed for three days straight. They were basically marooned in the hotel room, since they had neither friends nor transportation. They had never lived in snow country before and complained the entire time they were there. Jim's wife made it obvious that she did not want to be there. She bitched continually about having nothing to do and how she thought life sucked in an area where it continually snowed.

After three days stranded in the hotel, Jim called and insisted that he needed his car. He said he was promised that his car would be delivered and he wanted it right now. The fact that his wife was upset didn't help matters. On the fourth day in the hotel, Jim called and said he was going back home and would enroll in another school. I knew he was serious. I tried my best to placate him. I told him that I would rent them a car until Mr. Six could have his car transported. Jim was adamant about wanting his own car – not a rental.

"I want my car and I want it now!" Jim insisted. "This is bullshit! You guys told me I would have my car and a nice place to live. My wife and I are going back home."

I knew it was up to me to keep Jim in Boulder until school started and he could be officially enrolled. As a consequence, I spent more time with that couple than I ever anticipated. With no other students or players around campus, and with the heavy snow continuously falling, it was all I could do to keep shuffling them from movies, to lunches and then to dinners. The real problem was Jim's wife. It appeared that she never wanted to come to Colorado in the first place and so she seized every opportunity to blame her husband for the current predicament.

I called Crowder and told him that I was afraid we were going to lose Clay. "He can't get into the married student housing until school re-opens," I told him. "They're stuck in the hotel and have nothing to do." I also mentioned that Six had promised to have their car transported to Colorado, but that had not yet happened.

Crowder told me to call Six and find out what the hold up was in having Clay's car transported to Colorado.

When I reached Six I said, "They have been stuck in a hotel for five days with no transportation. They are constantly complaining about living in a hotel with nothing to do but watch TV. And to top it off, it has been snowing the whole time they have been here."

"Okay, relax," Six told me. "Get them a suite at the Hyatt House today and tell them they can stay there until they can move into the student housing apartments. Be sure they have everything they need in their room. The presidential suite is good; I have stayed there a number of times. Tell them to use room service and order anything they want. Put the room under my name; I have an account there."

"We can't do that," I explained. "The NCAA doesn't allow for such expensive housing."

"Bob, shut the fuck up and do what I say," he quickly replied. "What else seems to be the problem with them?"

"Well, they want their car," I replied. "I tried to get them a rental but they're insisting on driving their own car. When do you think you can have theirs here?" I asked.

Six put me on hold while he placed another call. When he returned, Six asked me, "Where is the car now?"

"It's at his father's house in Los Angeles."

"Okay, tell him he will have it soon," Six said.

"How soon, Mr. Six?" I asked.

"I'll have it there by 6 this evening," he replied. "You take him to the airport to pick it up."

I was utterly confused. It was not possible to get Jim's car from California to Denver in less than six hours. "Do you mean today?" I asked.

"Yes. Tonight at 6 your time," he assured me.

Six then gave me instructions to go to the Continental Airlines' hanger at the Denver airport and get the car there. He said that he was shipping it on a cargo plane from LA.

Sure enough, when Jim and I got to the airport, the cargo plane was just landing. We watched as the cargo door opened and out came Jim's car.

The next day I went to the Hyatt House. Jim and his wife had checked out and were on their way back to California in their own car. I never saw or talked to him again. I heard that he enrolled and played at the University of Oregon.

Postscript

Bob Six was CEO of Continental Airlines from 1936 to 1981. For many years he was one of the biggest and best supporters of Colorado football. Even though he never attended CU, he developed a strong passion for our football program. He was gruff, determined, and a scrappy risk-taker which paid off for the airline that he built and forged in his own image. He was married twice - first to Ethel Merman and subsequently to Audrey Meadows, both successful actresses.

* * *

Home Visits
– Surviving the Big Apple –

In his hit rendition of *New York, New York*, Frank Sinatra sings:
Start spreading the news, I'm leaving today.
*I want to be a part of it - New York, New York.**
Now I am sure there are many wonderful things about New York City, but let me share what happened on one particular recruiting trip I made to the "Big Apple."

It was 1980, I was coaching at the University of Colorado and was recruiting a big lineman from Butler Junior College in Kansas, by the name of Buster Vaughn. Buster stood 6'4" and weighed 290 pounds. He wasn't a great player but I thought he was good enough to play in the Big 8 Conference. He was also being recruited by the University of Kansas, Kansas State University, and Oklahoma State University, among others.

It has always been my practice to make a home visit with each player I was recruiting. Despite attending a junior college in Kansas, Buster's home was actually in New York City. I scheduled a date to meet with his family. The plan was to fly to New York City and visit with his family during Christmas vacation. I told him that I would call a couple days before the scheduled date to get directions to his home.

As promised, I phoned Buster two days before the scheduled meeting. "I will be flying into LaGuardia Airport on Wednesday," I informed him. "I'll get a room near the airport, rent a car and be at your place by 7 p.m. So, please give me driving directions to your place from LaGuardia."

"Here, I'll let you talk to my dad," Buster replied.

Mr. Vaughn got on the telephone. "Coach, we'll pick you up at your hotel."

"No, that really isn't necessary," I said. "Just give me directions and I'll find my way there."

Mr. Vaughn stated forcefully, "We live in Harlem and I don't think it is safe for you to drive here by yourself. Buster and I will pick you up and then take you back to your hotel after the visit. And don't eat dinner. My wife is cooking. Ribs sound okay?"

"Okay," I replied. Not having to rent a car and buy dinner would save the school some money. I told Mr. Vaughn I would meet them in the hotel lobby at 6:30 p.m.

I traveled light, bringing only one bag and my briefcase, both as carry-ons. My wallet was inside the briefcase. When I got off the plane at LaGuardia, I found an empty counter, opened my briefcase, and retrieved my hotel reservation papers. Then I went to the restroom.

By now, it was almost 3 p.m. I had been on the plane for over three hours and thought it wise to freshen up. While using the urinal, I set my two pieces of luggage down where I could watch them out of the corner of my eye.

I was taking care of business when I saw a guy grab my briefcase and head for the door. "Hey!" I shouted. "What the hell do you think you're doing?"

I pulled back from the urinal and ran after the thief, yelling and screaming like a banshee while awkwardly trying to zip up my pants at the same time. I chased him down the hall until a young woman ran smack into me and we both tumbled head-over-heels to the floor of the terminal. The culprit disappeared, along with my briefcase and wallet. I never saw him again. I later learned that the woman was an accomplice, strategically placed to detain the victim, in this case – me.

Two policemen appeared to identify the source of all the commotion. I explained what had happened. They looked at each other and shook their heads, obviously thinking I was some sort of country bumpkin. They explained the usual scenario of a thief working with an accomplice – an obviously successful strategy designed to allow the perpetrator adequate time to escape. The cops asked me to go with them to give a statement. I replied that first I needed to return to the men's room to retrieve my other bag. They exchanged another of those "I-can't-believe-this-guy" looks with one another. When I returned to the restroom, sure enough, my other bag was gone as well.

After I had finished giving my statement to the police, I caught a taxi to the hotel in preparation for my upcoming meeting with the Vaughn family. I mentioned to the driver that my baggage had been stolen. He told me that the airport was a high-crime area and that thieves especially like to take advantage of visitors to the "Big Apple."

My taxi fare to the hotel was $33.75. Fortunately, I had $275 cash in my pocket. With a $9 tip I figured I was still saving the college money, inasmuch as it would have cost twice as much if I had rented a car. However, my ego was somewhat deflated when the bellman heard the price. "$42!" he exclaimed. "Why did you pay $42?"

I stammered and stuttered but failed to come up with a plausible answer. He railed on, "The airport is only six miles from here; your fare should have been only $12 or so." No way around it - the cab driver screwed me and took advantage of the fact I didn't know how far the hotel was from the airport.

As if to rub salt in the wound, the bellman suggested that instead of taking a taxi back to the airport, I should take the free airport shuttle, which I also could have taken to get to the hotel in the first place. "Oh well," I told him. "At least I'll save the $42 I expected to pay for the return trip to the airport!"

I called my secretary and asked her to cancel my credit card. The bellman assured me he would file a complaint with the taxi company.

The hotel was definitely not a five-star facility, on the other hand, it was clean and the staff was very helpful in getting me checked-in. I bought a toothbrush, razor, and shaving cream at the lobby store. After I paid for the toiletries, I felt like I was robbed for the third time that day.

I went down to the lobby at 6:30 p.m. Buster, his dad, and an older brother were already there waiting for me. All three men were huge. Buster was the smallest of the three. His dad and brother were both taller and probably outweighed him by 40 to 50 pounds.

The four of us squeezed into a station wagon and headed towards Harlem. I was amazed at the level of poverty I saw as we got closer to their apartment complex. We parked the car on the street and as we got out, Mr. Vaughn directed me to walk in the middle, between his sons. I wasn't really scared - after all I was with three guys who looked like they could all play in the NFL - but I was a little concerned. Here I was – a white guy in a suit – walking around Harlem at night. That probably doesn't happen all that often.

We passed five guys who openly stared as we walked past them to the apartment. They were all standing around a barrel that had a fire in it, trying to keep warm. As we approached the outside stairwell leading to the second story apartment, three other black men approached us with attitudes that made me feel even more uncomfortable. One asked Mr. Vaughn, "Is everything all right, Willie?"

"Yeah," Mr. Vaughn replied. "This is a ball coach from Colorado wanting to talk with Alva and me about Buster. Everything is cool."

As we walked up the rickety wooden stairs, I noticed some red spots on each step. I am not certain what those red spots actually were, but they sure looked like blood to me. Each step had a few of these red blotches which made me think that someone had recently lost blood, on the very same staircase I was now using.

Shit, I thought to myself. *What the hell am I doing here?* I could have met the entire family at some nice restaurant and not screwed with this situation.

I felt much better once we reached their apartment. It was very clean and comfortable and Buster's mother, Alva, had prepared a wonderful dinner. We ate and talked for about two hours, after which, Mr. Vaughn and Buster took me back to the hotel.

Back at the hotel, I bought a paper, got into the elevator, and headed for my room on the third floor. As I left the elevator and started down the hall to my room, I noticed a man walking towards me. He was a white male wearing a blue jacket and a very wrinkled pair of beige slacks. As our eyes met, we both said, "Good evening," and continued on. I don't know why, but as we passed I turned to look back at him. I think maybe I was amazed at how wrinkled his pants were and wanted one last look.

I was surprised to see that the guy had also stopped and had turned back towards me. He had a black object in his hand which I could see as he raised his arm, ready to hit me. My reflexes caused me to raise my arm in self-defense, to ward off the blow I was about to receive from this son-of-a-bitch. He struck my raised arm, just below my elbow. I responded with a punch to his temple. He went down with a look of total surprise. My left arm was killing me but my adrenaline had kicked in and I proceeded to punch and kick the bastard as he tried to get up. I hit him a few good shots; you can tell when you really connect with one.

As I was yelling, screaming, and punching, he rolled around on the hallway floor, attempting to get away. He had no fight in him. I continued to punch away hoping that I could knock him unconscious. I remember thinking that I hoped he didn't also have an accomplice.

All the noise and ruckus soon brought out the other guests on the floor, curious to see what was happening. Since I was beating the guy while he was apparently helpless on the floor, I obviously looked like the bad guy. Two guys and a woman came to the guy's rescue by grabbing me and wrestling me up against the wall, despite my loud protests. I told them that I was the victim and that he was the bad guy, attempting to rob me. They were not convinced. As they held me, the little prick who started all this, stumbled to his feet, ran to the stairwell, and disappeared.

What a day. As I finally got into bed at 3 a.m., I reflected on the day and remembered the lyrics:

These vagabond shoes, are longing to stray,

*Right through the very heart of it – New York, New York.**

That's what you think, Sinatra.

Postscript

Buster did enroll at the University of Colorado and, to my surprise, the hotel comped my room. A week later I received a letter from the taxi company apologizing for the blatant overcharge. The letter went on to say that they hoped the refund check they left for me at the hotel was adequate compensation. I never got the check. I bet the bellman cashed it.

* *New York, New York* lyrics by Fred Ebb and John Kander

4

Trap Game Adventures

– Wimps, Whining and Winning –

Two things were guaranteed at the Rocky Mountain and Mid-America conferences - beautiful scenery and crappy weather. These two seemed to go hand-in-hand. Of course, not every game was played in a foot of snow, but I'll be danged if we didn't have at least one every year.

Nineteen ninety-four was no different. I was the head coach at Fort Hays State College and we had a really good team. It was the first week of November — prime time for bad weather — and my team was facing a "trap" game, a game where over-confidence could jeopardize what should be an easy win.

Every team has a trap game. Ours was the Colorado School of Mines. Throughout my career, I was known as a grind-it-out coach. My teams had to operate on all cylinders to win ball games; that is to say, there was no such thing as a "sure victory." This time I had a feeling we were taking our opponent too lightly. Lose this game and we could watch our playoff hopes go down the drain.

Twelve years as a high school coach combined with the knowledge I gained from Coach Bill Mallory during my time at Colorado, convinced me that the practice on the day before the game was the one that mattered most. It was the one that set the tone for the game. It was where we went over the minute details that we may have not spent enough time on during the week. We also made sure everyone knew their tasks on special teams.

As we rolled into Golden, Colorado, on a Friday afternoon we were welcomed with four-foot snow drifts and new snow was still falling.

"Guess there's no pre-game day practice," I overheard one of my players say. "Surely Coach won't make us practice in this crap."

"Oh, we're going to practice," I yelled, attempting to get my team's attention. "Stop acting like a bunch of babies. We have to play in this crap tomorrow and I have a few things I want to go over to make sure we win the game tomorrow. The bus leaves for the practice field in 45 minutes. Be sure to bundle up."

The Colorado School of Mines had a first-class athletic department. Marv Kay was the head football coach as well as the athletic director. Marv was a great guy who at one time was elected mayor of Golden, Colorado. As soon as he heard that we wanted to practice, Marv had the field cleared to make it more accessible. Marv is truly a better man than I in that regard; there is no way I would have obliged had the tables been turned.

As the bus struggled up the hill to the practice field, our driver stopped the vehicle. "I can't go any further," he said, "unless you guys wanna push this son-of-a-bitch back up this hill. We're about to get stuck."

The fact that we were 300 yards from the field made little difference to me, but the players were not so happy.

"Coach, I can't feel my knees," one of the players complained, as we all trudged through the deep snow.

"Quit whining like a bunch of babies," I snapped, although he was probably telling me the truth. The snow was waist-deep in some parts and the temperature was about 10 degrees. Once we finally arrived at the playing field, the players huddled up like cattle and were doing nothing but bitching and complaining.

My defensive coordinator, Tim O'Connor, came up to me and softly whispered, "Coach, the players are cold and really not into practicing. I think we have all the details ready for the game tomorrow. I know we are ready to go defensively."

I looked around to survey the situation. I saw my players shivering and hugging themselves, and thought about how it could be colder tomorrow. My team looked like a bunch of wimps and all I could think about was our letting the weather affect the outcome of the game.

"Enough!" I screamed. And then in a moment of high-drama and frustration, I ripped off my jacket and my shirt. There I was, bare-chested in the snow, trying to make a point. It might have been cold but I had so much adrenaline flowing through my body that it didn't bother me. "Now let's get to work!"

The players and the staff looked at me in shock. I had gotten their attention. They worked their asses off for 45 minutes—not because they wanted to—but mainly out of fear, fear of what I would do if they didn't work. For a group that looked and sounded like a bunch of pansies just minutes before, they sure toughened up in a hurry.

Fear is a great motivator. Fear of losing was the reason for my outlandish behavior; fear of losing my respect was the reason they kept going.

After practice I pulled my shirt back on and called the team together. "Listen men," I began. "Tomorrow's game is huge. Our playoff hopes hinge on this game. We need to win and we can't blame the weather as the reason why we don't. Screw the cold and the snow! Let's get ready for a victory!"

As I was talking to the players I noticed a small hill leading back to the bus, which was parked some 300 yards away. I thought I would lighten the mood by sprinting down the hill, then jumping and sliding on my belly atop the snow towards the bus. I had one of the players break us down with the usual huddle and chants, and then I immediately broke off into my sprint - thinking that the size of the slope would enable me to slide roughly 30 yards in the direction of the bus.

Once at top speed — keep in mind that the snow was deep and my top speed wasn't very fast — I straightened my body and jumped face-first. The glorious ride down the hill that I had envisioned was replaced by a swift and startling plunk. I must have looked like a javelin sinking into the ground. I couldn't move, let alone see anything.

What in the hell have I just done? I wondered.

Moments later I heard the pounding of cleats rushing up to me. No laughter, just panic. My players thought I had injured myself. Fortunately, I emerged from the snow unharmed and fully intact— except for my prescription sunglasses, which I have not found to this day.

* * *

Postscript

We won the game the next day 34-14, confirming my belief that the final practice prior to the game is the most important one.

5

Jogging Down the Highway

– A Road Trip Tradition –

"Get up, men!" I yelled. Half-asleep players groaned. "Time to wake up and get ready for our lunch-time jog," I announced. More groans. I was head football coach at Mesa State College at Grand Junction, Colorado. We were on a bus headed to Las Vegas, New Mexico, for a conference game against New Mexico Highlands University. Early in my coaching career, I learned that long bus trips the day before a game equaled potential disaster—tired bodies and tired minds on game day. So in order to get the juices flowing, I would ask the bus driver to stop the vehicle about half-way through a trip, offload the players, and make them jog for a mile.

This didn't make me popular with the players, but it seemed to work. Twelve minutes of running was certainly better conditioning than 10 to 12 unbroken hours of doing nothing but sleep, listen to music, watch videos, eat, or play cards on a team bus.

The Rocky Mountain Athletic Conference didn't provide many short trips. Besides the 10 to 12 hour jaunts, some of the non-conference, road trips ran 15 to 16 hours or more. They were tough on the body, especially the day before a game.

It was quite a sight to be in the middle of nowhere and see 42 players, all dressed in the same school-issued gear—sweat suit, shorts and t-shirt—jogging down the side of the road. We got a lot of strange looks from people driving by.

On this particular day, a scorching September afternoon, my veteran players knew what awaited them. Courtney DeBruin, sports writer for *The Grand Junction Sentinel,* accompanied us on this trip. For some reason, he wanted to ride on the team bus. I was a little surprised because Courtney normally didn't ride with the team. Since I knew I didn't want him bothering my players during this long trip, I assigned him a seat up front, right next to me.

While making small talk with Courtney, I asked, "So, what sports did you play when you were younger?" Courtney stood about 6'2". He was a tall, skinny man, who didn't look like an athlete. In fact, he didn't appear to have an athletic bone in his body. Not by football standards anyway.

"Well, I ran cross-country in high school," he said, "and I still run when I get a chance. Right now, I run about 30 miles a week so I can stay in shape for marathons."

That piqued my curiosity. And set me to thinking. I asked Courtney if he was any good.

"I finish in the top 25 percent on most occasions," Courtney responded.

Being aware that my players would bitch when we stopped for our lunch-time jog, I described the routine to Courtney and asked if he'd be interested in having some fun with the players. He said that he'd heard about my routine of running just before lunch and that he'd be glad to play along, commenting that he had planned to run with the players anyway.

When it came time for the run, we were in a desolate area, headed along highway I-25 somewhere in New Mexico. I motioned for the bus driver to pull over to the side of the highway.

The players groaned in typical fashion. "Come on, Coach, do we have to do this?"

"Yes," I yelled. "You guys know the drill, how many times do we have to go through this?"

A couple of the older players continued to complain. One of our team captains came up to me and asked, "Coach, it's really, really hot out there. Do we really have to?"

"Okay, okay," I said. "I've got an idea. Let's make it a race between champions, the way the ancient Greeks and Romans used to do, or David and Goliath in the Bible. The captains will pick a player to run and I'll pick someone to race against him. If your guy wins the race, nobody else has to run; but if my guy wins, your asses are mine, and everybody runs with no more bitching. Any questions?"

One of the team captains spoke. "Let me make sure I understand you. If our guy wins, we don't jog; if your guy wins, we all jog. Is that it?"

"That's it!" I said. It couldn't be any simpler than that.

The players went wild when they heard there was a chance they might not have to jog before lunch. You would have thought three coeds were running naked up and down the aisle.

When it came to picking their runner, the players knew exactly who they wanted. "Eric, Eric, Eric," they chanted. Eric Daniels was a senior slot back. In high school, he ran the mile for his track team. Whenever I had the players run laps around the practice field, Eric always finished first, and in a convincing fashion, often beating the others by 50 yards or more and lapping a few linesmen in doing so.

I looked around at the coaches, trainers, manager, and even the bus driver, trying to make it look like I was hunting for a runner to compete for me. The bus driver was an older guy, who was very much overweight.

"I need to find someone outside the football family," I said.

"I don't want to have someone run who you guys can influence to throw the race or hold it against them if they win. Obviously, the bus driver is out." I paused, looked around for dramatic effect, and then continued, "That only leaves me with one other choice, Courtney, the sports writer – if he would even agree to do it." I paused again, as if reconsidering, then shook my head, and said, "I really don't think this is a good idea after all; you guys get ready to run."

The players went berserk. They were all yelling and screaming for us to have the race. Some of the players even went up to Courtney and told him if he agreed to run the race they would mow his lawn for a month. Courtney played along and told me he would try, even though he lived in an apartment and didn't have any lawn to be mowed.

So the race was on.

None of the players knew that they were being played the entire time. The players thought that the best distance runner on the team was taking on a non-athletic desk jock; it would be no contest. Eric was the hands-on favorite. *No running on this trip*, they thought.

Eric and Courtney got out of the bus and stretched nervously on the side of the road. I asked the bus driver to pull one mile down the road - and the race began.

During the first half-mile, the two runners seemed to be pacing themselves and were even talking to one another as they leisurely jogged down the highway. About three-quarters of the way, Eric picked up the pace and started running a bit faster. To his surprise, Courtney remained right beside him. I could see Eric looking over at Courtney and could only imagine his disappointment in not being able to shake the sports writer.

With 300 yards remaining, Eric started running faster, but to no avail - he could not pull in front of Courtney. When they hit the last 100 yards, I could see Eric starting to tire while Courtney looked like he was just warming up. *That's my boy*, I said to myself. The players, who were now standing outside of the bus, started running towards the two runners, shouting encouragement for Eric. Courtney then started his sprint to the finish line, beating his opponent by nearly 25 yards. "Okay you guys, line up to do your mile," I cheerfully directed.

Eric, the coaches, and I then got back onto the bus and drove the mile down the highway to wait for the grumbling and complaining players to complete their jog. Courtney ran with them.

* * *

Postscript

Following the lunch-time jog down I-25, we stopped for lunch at a rest stop. I noticed that during lunch, Eric sat alone. I am not sure if he was being blackballed by the players for losing the race or if he was mad at himself for not winning. And yes, we won the game the next day.

6

Clowns and Accomplices

– A Break in the Monotony –

Every team has a clown or two. Some are would-be court jesters, others are just frustrated comedians. We had our share at Mesa State College. Having someone who likes to pull pranks, or keep the coaches and their teammates laughing, is as important to team chemistry as snow is to reindeers. Allowing someone to break up certain tense situations, or the monotony of football, is okay, as long as it doesn't totally destroy the focus needed at the time.

In 1984, our returning Mesa State College team was loaded with great athletes. I knew we had everything needed to be successful with the possible exception of toughness. Great athletes without toughness could mean disaster to a team. Early in the season it appeared that the players were well aware of their potential but lacked the aggressiveness all great teams need. On the third day of practice, during an "Oklahoma Drill," which pits one offensive player against one defensive player, man-on-man, I blew my whistle and gathered all the players around me. I was pissed and I wanted them all to know it.

"This is BULLSHIT," I yelled. "This team lacks toughness and I won't stand for that. We have no one out here that has any prick.

We've been out here three full days and I haven't seen anyone show me he has the toughness I am looking for," I continued to yell. "We haven't even had a fight amongst ourselves. I have never, ever been around a team that at sometime during two-a-days hasn't gotten involved in a fight or two. Competitive, tough guys usually get pissed sometime during practice and make their stand by not allowing a teammate to push them around. You are all practicing for a starting position." Once again I yelled, "BULLSHIT" and walked away.

During the next morning's coaches' staff meeting, one of our student coaches, who lived in the dorm, asked to speak. Since he played on the team last season, he was still close to many of this year's team members.

"Coach, I don't want to seem like a tattletale," he said, "but last night I overheard Ken Marchiol talking with the team and planning a fake fight for practice today." Ken was a junior and a very good player. He was a guy with some inner toughness. He was also a bit of a team clown. Once he completely taped a freshman from his hometown of Trinidad, Colorado, to a weight machine. He told the young player that if he didn't spend more time in the weight room, he had better not tell anyone that they had gone to the same high school.

"Don't disgrace me," he warned the young player.

"What are you talking about?" I asked the student coach.

"Well, since you challenged the team's toughness," he continued, "Ken and some of the seniors thought they would get two players to fake a fight and turn it into an offense vs. defense free-for-all. All the players would join in and pretend that they were actually mad and fake fight with each other. Ken said, 'That should make the old bastard happy.'"

We finished our meeting with the plan being that the coaches would just let the players do their thing. We would break up any fights and play it by ear. The major thing I was concerned about was that we didn't waste too much practice time with this kind of tom-foolery.

Practice was uneventful that afternoon until we got into a live scrimmage. About two-thirds of the way into the drill, the players' secret plan exploded. The offense ran a sweep around our defensive end, which just happened to be where Ken Marchiol was playing. As the whistle blew to stop the play, Ken and offensive lineman Joe Cotroneo began yelling at each other. Ken accused Joe of holding on the play and was visibly upset because he was not able to make the tackle on the play. Joe responded with something like, "Why don't you stop crying and go screw yourself."

Ken grabbed Joe and the fight was on—offensive players against defensive players. It was easy to tell them apart because offensive players were wearing dark blue jerseys, while defense wore white. Fights broke out with sides being chosen by the color of the shirt they were wearing. Usually I was slow at breaking up any fights during practice. It's a natural thing for aggressive, macho players to periodically blow their cool and just haul off and hit someone. I never saw anybody get hurt during a fight at practice, since of course they were all wearing pads and helmets. I let this fight go on a little longer than usual, since I knew it was a "fake" fight.

I was surprised at the ferocity out there on the field. The players made it look like a real free-for-all. They were punching and jumping on each other just as they might do in a real brawl. After two or three minutes I finally had enough and started yelling and blowing my whistle. As the players started to settle down, I heard more yelling and arguing but this time it was between two of my coaches. Bill Kralicek, an offensive coach and Sheldon Keresey, a defensive coach, were arguing about the fact the offense is always holding the defense.

"You S.O.B.'s are always holding us," Sheldon shouted at Bill.

"Screw you," Bill replied.

The players were now paying close attention as the two coaches squared off. Bill, who was bigger than Sheldon, went up to him and pushed him slightly in the chest, saying "You pussies are always bitching about something. Just get your guys to play some ball and keep their mouths shut!"

Sheldon didn't back down and said, "I saw Joe hold Ken and I am sick of the offense thinking there are no rules during practice!"

The commotion between the two coaches got to the players. Joe and Ken went up to their respective coaches and tried to calm them down. Sheldon pushed Ken aside saying, "I'm sick of them holding you!"

Before I could get in between the two angry coaches, Sheldon grabbed Bill's arm as he started walking away and tried to turn him around. To the surprise of all, Bill turned and landed a solid punch in Sheldon's face. Blood squirted from Sheldon's mouth and I swear I saw a tooth come flying out. Not only was I in shock, but the players were as well. The players were silent and couldn't believe that two coaches were involved in a fight. No one said a word.

I started toward Bill knowing if he was out of control he could crush me with a single blow. Bill was an All Big Eight offensive guard at the University of Colorado. He was also the heavy weight wrestler for the school's varsity team. He was one of the most powerful men I have ever known. I was hoping his respect for me as the head coach would enable me to control him. As I approached him, he started laughing. Out of the corner of my eyes I could see Sheldon also laughing. I started to realize that something was up.

Unbeknownst to me, Bill and Sheldon thought they would stage a fight of their own. Like the players, they did a good job convincing all of us that it was real. The blood I saw coming out of Sheldon's mouth was actually a capsule filled with red dye. It was quite realistic. By now, the players and coaches were all giggling and laughing. Everyone thought it was cool that the two coaches had turned the tables on the players by staging their own fight.

I pretended I was upset with not only the players but the coaches as well. "Cut the bullshit and let's get back to work," I yelled. I thought it was good for the team to have some fun together but wanted all involved to understand I was a no-nonsense guy and playing football was what I was all about.

*   *   *

Postscript

We won 10 games that season.

7

Obey the Law

– *Don't Tamper with the U.S. Mail* –

"That's the game! Final score: Mesa State 14, Southern Colorado 14." I cringed as the mournful voice of the announcer echoed across the stadium and bounced off the hard backs of the rapidly emptying seats.

Dissatisfied with not getting a clear-cut victory, I stormed angrily off the field. Each step I took seemed harder than the one before and, no matter how fast I walked, I couldn't escape the biting barbs of Robert Mullen, Southern Colorado's first-year athletic director.

"I never thought I'd see the day when the great Bob Cortese would settle for a tie," Mullen mocked. It wasn't funny. I was tempted to smack him in the chops and wipe that shit-eating grin off his face. Right now, I didn't feel like talking to anyone from Southern Colorado—least of all, Mullen, USC's new athletic director. He was about to push me over the edge.

You see, I knew something about USC's athletic program that Mullen didn't and this information would turn his school's world upside down. Although to this day, I swear that was never my intention.

I looked him right in the eye and said, "You better keep your coach under control and not worry about Bob Cortese!"

Shocked, he said, "Excuse me?"

"You're lucky we didn't win today because, if we had won, I would have blown the whistle on your coach!"

Mullen seemed intrigued by this turn of events. Rumor had it that he had big plans for the future of his university. As a former basketball coach, Mullen dreamed of being athletic director at a top basketball school. He wanted USC basketball to compete at the NCAA Division I level; however, like Mesa State, USC didn't have a big enough budget. The only way Mullen could achieve his goal would be to drop a high-dollar sport and football seemed the most likely target.

However, before Mullen could eliminate the football program, he would first have to get rid of the one person who stood in his way—USC's popular football coach, Mike Friedman. That was easier said than done. Friedman was the school's face to the community. For many years, his teams had dominated the Rocky Mountain Athletic Conference.

Getting rid of Friedman would be difficult. Mullen worried that he may have picked the wrong fight with the wrong man at the wrong time. He would need to dig up some dirt on his nemesis. Moreover, he would need plenty of it if he were to successfully uproot this well-liked coach from Pueblo, Colorado.

"What are you talking about?" Mullen demanded when I shot off my mouth in anger that day. On the one hand, I ached to spill my guts but, on the other hand, I had made a promise to my staff, and myself, that I wouldn't tell anyone.

"Never mind," I said with a shrug as I made my way into the locker room.

I had no involvement in the events that subsequently took place, but suffice it to say that these are the things of which legends are made and before the dust settled, Mike Friedman and his entire staff were out of jobs. The scandal would make national sports headlines, including a brief blurb in *Sports Illustrated*.

The rivalry between Mesa and Southern Colorado had not always been this vitriolic. For many years, USC had been a perennial contender for the conference championship, while Mesa State languished near the bottom. I brought Mesa State up from the dregs of NAIA football to competing for the conference championship. In 1982, USC had been picked by the coaches and the media to win the RMAC while we were tabbed to finish second. Friedman could feel me breathing down his neck.

The rivalry reached an all-time high when I hired Joe Pannunzio to be my offensive coordinator. In 1981, Pannunzio had just finished his illustrious career at Southern Colorado and he called me, inquiring about a position that I had posted. I was somewhat surprised that he would call me, based on the animosity that existed between our two schools.

Both schools were located in great communities of 100,000, giving us each a big fan base. We were located in the same state and often competed for the same recruits, many times resulting in one of us hating the other just a little more.

After Pannunzio interviewed, I decided I wanted to hire him because he was a pretty sharp guy. I offered him the job, but I told him, "Whether you come here or not, we *are* going to win. My success does not hinge on your joining us. It's whether you want to join the bandwagon."

Pannunzio would later tell me that those words sold him on wanting to coach for me. Since being on my staff, Pannunzio has been at Ole Miss, TCU, Auburn, Kansas, the University of Miami, as well as head coach at Murray State. I could tell he had the pedigree to be a great coach when he was just 21-years old.

Pannunzio was loyal to me and he was loyal to our school. He earned my respect when he said, "I still have a soft spot in my heart for Pueblo, because I graduated from Pueblo and Coach Friedman was very good to me."

I respected Panunnzio for that. Even though I didn't like USC or Coach Friedman, I respected Panunnzio because he was loyal to his school and he was loyal to his coach. Loyalty was something I always appreciated.

A few weeks prior to the game, Coach Friedman called and talked with me about exchanging game film. The only problem was that video was just starting to be used instead of the more expensive 16 mm film. It all came down to cost efficiency. USC had money to burn. The cost was $500 to do a game film, not to mention it would take a couple of days after the game to get it printed and ready for use. Mesa State didn't have that type of money. We used a camcorder and transferred it to VHS videotapes. I'll admit, the video quality didn't compare to film, but you couldn't beat the price. Friedman was one of the lucky ones. When it came to breaking down games, 16 mm film was the Rolls Royce of the coaching profession.

"There is no way I'm trading film for video," Friedman said. "It's unfair. You get high quality film and all I get in return is this cheap video crap."

"Well, then let's not exchange," I said.

"No, we can still exchange," Friedman replied.

We decided that we would trade the video but, instead of him sending the film, he would video tape the film off his viewing screen and send me a copy on video. I considered it a fair trade.

A few days before the game, I went through my normal routine of breaking down our opponent. The video was okay, except there was one problem. Every time they lined up in a certain formation, there appeared to be dust on the lens and I couldn't see where all the players were. This was typical with film - you could just blow on the lens and then it would be okay. It happened from time to time so I didn't suspect any foul play, but it did seem to be one hell of a coincidence that it happened every time his team lined up in that formation.

This was big because, in Friedman's entire career, he only ran two offensive formations. He ran a wing offense and a wing to the field with a split end. It bugged me because here, out of nowhere, he had a new formation and we couldn't see it.

I went ahead and broke down the video thinking everything was fine.

The next day my assistant coaches, including Panunnzio, watched the film. After they finished, they came into my office.

"What do you think about the film, Coach?" Pannunzio asked.

"Other than when they lined up in that different formation, I thought it was fine," I answered.

"Did you hear what they were saying?" Panunnzio continued. I could tell that he was angry.

It was always my practice to turn off the volume when reviewing game video because crowd noise distracted me. My coaches were the opposite. When they broke down opponents, they always cranked up the sound. They thought it gave them a good idea of the environment we would be playing in.

"What the hell are you talking about?" I fired back.

"We gotta show you something, Coach," one of my other assistants said. They had left the film in the exact spot where USC was lined up in the weird formation. Only this time, the volume was tuned all the way up.

They pushed "play" and what I heard on that tape left me dumbfounded. "This should really fuck Cortese up," one of the USC assistants boasted.

Another stated, through a lot of laughter, "Not knowing where these guys are lined up is really going to screw them up. They'll have to figure out during the game how to line up against us and they won't be able to practice it during the week."

All of this was on the film and I was pissed. In addition, they were taking a string and wiggling it in front of the lens; it wasn't dust as I had earlier suspected.

"That no good son-of-a-bitch," I yelled.

"You should call the RMAC offices right now and file a complaint," one of my assistants suggested.

"Why don't you get Friedman on the phone right now and tell that bastard we know they doctored the film?" said another.

Pannunzio sat in disbelief that the school he loved could stoop so low. "I can't believe it," he said. "No way!"

The jackasses at USC didn't work with camcorders very often and, hence, they failed to realize that the device had an internal microphone that was on all of the time. Therefore, even though they thought they were taping a silent film, their comments were none-the-less being recorded by the camcorder.

I decided that I wouldn't say anything about it unless we won the game because I didn't want to sound like a crybaby. However, if we won, I was going to tell my story to all who would listen. I would say, "We won, but I just want you to know they cheated. They doctored the game film." I didn't want to make a big deal of it; I just wanted to keep it quiet and file it in the back of my mind.

The night before the game, we had our coaches' meeting. This is where all our game decisions are made. If we win the toss, do we take the ball or defer? Which direction is the wind going to be coming from? If we score late, do we kick the PAT or do we go for the win with a two-point conversion? We figured it was best to make the big decisions before the game took place, rather than burning timeouts and making decisions under pressure.

USC had already lost a conference game while we were undefeated. We decided that, if it came down to kicking an extra point to tie, or going for two, we would settle for the tie, because we probably wouldn't lose another game. A tie would give us the RMAC title and send us into the national playoffs—assuming, of course, that we took care of our remaining schedule.

Game day arrived. It was Saturday night in Pueblo, Colorado. It was the game of the week, with a cable station airing the game statewide.

Irv Brown, one of my dearest friends at the time, was doing "color" for the game. At that time he had been in talk radio for over 30 years and was beloved by a great listening audience. I had coached his two sons, Greg and Mike. Despite our close and long-standing relationship, I didn't let him know about the film-doctoring incident.

With 2:45 left in the game, we trailed 14-7, we had the ball and I felt that we had the momentum to win the game. It was a tough battle and both teams were playing very hard.

Russ Hodgson, a two-time All-American running back, carried the ball 12 times in a row.

"We should take him out and give him a breather," Pannunzio said to me from the press box, through my headset.

Russ came over to the sidelines. I turned him around, pushed him back onto the field and said, "You, playing tired, are better than any backups that I have over here."

We took a timeout and Russ started throwing up on the field. He was a tough *hombre*, our version of Earl Campbell. Like Earl Campbell, he was just one of those guys who looked tired but, once in possession of the football, he was going to run.

After we finally scored our second touchdown, bringing the score to 14-13, everyone in the stadium speculated on whether we were going to rush for the two-point win or kick the PAT for a one-point tie.

"Bob Cortese is never going to settle for the tie," Irv told a state-wide audience. "I promise you that."

However, this had already been decided late the night before at the coaches' meeting. We knew we would have the upper hand at winning the conference title. Besides, at the time we scored, we had two time-outs and I thought we would get the ball back with enough time to get within range and kick a three-point game-winning field goal.

We did get the ball back but, unfortunately, with only 15 seconds remaining. The game clock ran out before we were able to move the ball downfield far enough to attempt the field goal.

As we headed to the locker room, Robert Mullen, the USC athletic director, approached me and I made the comments that would eventually result in the monumental change at USC. Now remember, this is the guy who it was speculated wanted to drop football from his program.

The next day my athletic director, Jay Jefferson, came into my office and closed the door. Apparently, he had received a call from Mullen who questioned him about my comments. He said, "If Bob Cortese has a complaint about our coaches or our school, then he better spit it out or keep his mouth shut."

"What did you mean when you told him that?" Jay asked.

"I'll tell you the story only if you agree to drop it," I replied.

He agreed, so I filled him in on the film-doctoring incident. The next day, Jay came calling again. Apparently, USC's president had called Mesa State's president.

"We have to tell him about the film exchange," Jay said.

I argued, "We tied. The game is over; these things happen in coaching."

He was not dissuaded. After several minutes of trying to talk him out of it, I threw in the towel. "Go ahead, I can't stop you," I said. "If USC's president wants to know what happened, that's what happened."

Three days later, Jay was back in my office.

"Mullen talked with Coach Friedman and he denied anything ever happened," Jay said. "Mullen wants to see the tape." I really didn't want to do it, but it wasn't up to me. I had to mail a copy of the tape to Mullen.

When Joe Pannunzio learned what was going on, he asked if he could at least call his former coach and advise him that we were sending the tape to the athletic director. He wanted to give Friedman a heads-up about what might be coming down.

"Okay, sure," I said.

We mailed the tape to Mullen's office after we made a copy to keep for our records. Two days later, he called me. "Bob, I don't see or hear anything out of the ordinary."

"Are you sure? You don't hear the laughter of the coaches on the tape?" I asked.

"Bullshit. It didn't happen. There's no evidence," he said.

As we continued to talk, I reasoned that perhaps my assistants, who had made the copy, didn't leave the sound on when they were dubbing. But after five minutes of bickering back and forth, Mullen started to believe me.

"Have a copy sent to my home address so I can see the tape," he said.

We learned later that when Panunnzio told them we were sending a tape to Mullen, two of their coaches broke into the mailroom and opened his mail. They took out our copy of the tape and replaced it with another copy that they had duped – one that hadn't been doctored – sealed it back up and left it in the mailroom. That's a federal offense.

Mullen received the new copy which was delivered to his home, saw the evidence, and then the shit hit the fan. Friedman had dug the hole himself. The tape we sent Mullen provided the dirt he needed to get rid of the popular coach.

It was the biggest news in Colorado at that time. It made headlines in *The Denver Post*, as well as in the Grand Junction and Pueblo media outlets. It was everywhere. At the end of the season, Coach Friedman was fired.

Two years later, Southern Colorado dropped its football program. With Coach Friedman there, they would never have dropped football; he was too big in the community - at least too big for Mullen, who was still new. It was hard on the community. The team attracted big crowds, had state-of-the-art facilities, and they rewarded the community by winning. Now, all of a sudden the program was gone.

All because of a doctored film.

* * *

Postscript

Twenty-eight years after the film incident, USC is reviving its football program. In so doing, USC has gone back to its roots, as Friedman's old quarterback John Wristen—an honorable mention All-American—is now the head coach. Mullen's stay at USC was only five years and he never got his Division I basketball program. He is now the athletic director at UMASS—Fordham, where, ironically, he has added a football program.

8

The Arvada Era

My years as head coach at Arvada High School, in Arvada, Colorado, were successful due to my good fortune in having both great players and a great coaching staff. The following stories focus on Dan Patterson, a young and conscientious defensive coordinator, Bill Schoepflin, one of our best players, Mary Gillach, one of my biggest coaching surprises, and an equipment manager with a craving.

* * *

The Art of Compromise
— But I Knew I Was Right —

It was late Sunday evening December 3, 1976. I was hashing out plans with my coaches for the state championship game against Ranum High School in Westminster, Colorado. This night, we were working even later than usual, partly because we were getting ready to play for the state championship against a team that had very good players, and partly because they ran the potent and not-very-often seen old Wing-T offense. Misdirection at its best. Not many teams ran the Wing-T back in 1976, so of course we never had a chance to play against it.

Arvada was 10-1 that season and had a very good team as well. Many players from that year's team went on to play college football. Our best player, Bill Schoephlin, was named *1976 Colorado High School Player-of-the-Year*. Unfortunately, Schoephlin separated his shoulder in our semi-final victory so we weren't sure if he could play in the big game. Undoubtedly, we would be a lesser team without him. More about Bill and the game later.

That Sunday was a real grind. It had been a long season and we were trying to devise a game plan that could win the state championship. Around 9 p.m., after about 12 grueling hours of strategizing, my staff and I were exhausted. Our biggest concern was defending against Ranum's high scoring offense and their use of the Wing-T formation which was full of misdirection plays. This formation relied on convincing the opponent of going one way and then running the opposite.

Our defense was straight-forward: read our keys and stay at home. We ran a 4-4 defense and since our four linebackers had very good speed, we could just fly to the football. We were a quick-flow team and won a great number of football games playing that way. However, quick-flow was not a good strategy against the more slowly-developing misdirection of the Wing-T.

My defensive coordinator was Dan Patterson, a bright young coach who had played for the University of Colorado. Dan understood discipline and toughness and since it had not been long since he had been a player himself, he was able to relate well with our current players.

Late into Sunday evening the coaches and I were still arguing about whether or not we should continue playing our normal 4-4 scheme, or if we should adjust and play more of a "60-front" using only two linebackers. In goal-line situations we would usually jump into a 60-front, so it wasn't a totally foreign concept. We had two linebackers who knew how to "put their hands in the dirt" which meant they knew how to play down as defensive linemen as well.

Dan argued for staying with the same 4-4 scheme. He wanted to go to the BIG DANCE with the defense that got us there. That theory had a great deal of merit. My opinion, however, was that playing against Ranum's Wing-T with a 4-4 defense was like going to a ballroom dance with jitterbug dancers. We were not accustomed to playing against this style of offense. Our defense would be required to play differently because of so much misdirection. I knew from experience that quick-flowing linebackers were not the way to stop misdirection offenses. Since Dan didn't have any experience going up against the Wing-T, he naturally did not agree.

Attempting to be diplomatic and not contradict Dan's reasoning, I kept emphasizing the need to adapt to this new set of circumstances. But Dan was young and very stubborn. "Dan, I promise you in one week we will not be able to get our linebackers to slow down and read through the guards to the fullback," I argued. "By playing a 60-front we will cover up their guards and tackles and force them to play against a defense they are not expecting. We will be able to get quicker penetration by using six down linemen. We can slant and angle better out of this front. Quick penetration always causes problems for that style of offense."

"Coach, don't panic," Dan responded. "Our players are smart and we'll coach them this week on how to read their keys and stay more at home. Relax."

The entire coaching staff was tired – especially me. After 12 hours watching film and trying to devise our plan, we all needed

some sleep. "Fatigue makes cowards of us all," Coach Vince Lombardi reportedly said at one point during his career. How true it was
that evening! I was tired and didn't feel like arguing anymore. So I
gave in to Dan's argument.

"Okay, let's go home," I said. I still felt like we were making a big
mistake. Fatigue made me violate my own well-established coaching philosophy. I always believed that I should listen carefully to what
my assistant coaches advised but when their opinions were contrary
to what I believed, then I should go with what I felt was right. I always
said, "If I am going to get fired for losing, I want to get fired because I
was stupid, not because my assistants were stupid."

The game was set for Saturday at Folsom Stadium, home of the
University of Colorado Buffaloes - the same field where I played
during my college career. I thought it would be an advantage to play
at my alma mater since I was so familiar with the people and the environment. And what a thrill to play a high school game in a 50,000-
seat stadium!

We were allowed to practice on the Buff's artificial surface on
Tuesday and Wednesday of game week. This would be Arvada's
first time to play on a synthetic-grassed field. No problem! Ranum
hadn't played on one either. On Tuesday, while we were preparing
our scout team to run Ranums' offense against our defense, I decided I would play scout quarterback. I didn't think our scout team
quarterback could understand the integral steps that the opposing
quarterback would use while running their offense. After watching
a great deal of film, I understood how he opened up, faked the ball,
and executed as they ran their plays. I knew it would be critical for
our defense to get a good look.

After running four plays, I was scheduled to run a bootleg from
the quarterback position. I faked to the fullback, then to the halfback, and started to sprint (or what I thought was a sprint) around

our defensive end. POP! I felt a sharp pain in the back of my 34-year-old right leg and knew I had snapped my ham string. I went down like a ton of bricks. Boy, did it hurt. While the trainer worked on my leg, I thought how ironic it was that the worst injury I ever incurred on this field, happened as I was playing scout team quarterback for a high school team. I had played against some of the best college teams in the country on this same field and had never gotten an injury as serious as a torn ham string. I was finished playing scout team quarterback and went back to coaching.

During the next two practices, Dan did a good job making sure our defensive players understood what we were going to be up against. As I watched from the sideline, I still wasn't sure we were planning to use the correct defense. For Thursday's practice, I scheduled a 15 minute period using our 60-front, just in case Dan's scheme fell apart. Dan wasn't very happy about giving up that amount of defensive practice time for something he thought we would not use on Saturday, but he was a loyal soldier and even though I was injured, I was still the head coach.

Game day. The crowd was estimated at 6,000 and evenly split between the two schools. We received the opening kickoff and, on our first series of downs, went three and out having to punt from our 42-yard line. Ranum got the ball on their own 26-yard line. Their first play was a trap by the fullback right up the middle of our 4-4 defense. Bang - our inside middle linebacker met him at the line of scrimmage and tackled him for a one-yard gain. Our players were fired up and started jumping and cheering. I looked at Dan and he glanced back at me with a look that said, *I told you we were going to be fine.*

The next play Ranum ran was a counter to the halfback. Plus six yards. Then they ran a bootleg and caught our back side defensive end getting too nosy as their gifted quarterback scampered for nine more yards. A sweep for seven, another sweep for four, and they were in our territory. They continued down the field ripping our defense over and over again until they scored the first touchdown of the game. Our bus wasn't even cold yet and we were down 7-0.

Way too easy, I thought. No team that year marched the ball down the field on us like they did. Our players were in shock and were obviously confused. Dan and the rest of our defensive staff brought them together as they came off the field and tried to settle them down. I wasn't able to hear what he told them because I had to start calling plays for our offense. I felt comfortable he would make some corrections.

After returning the ensuing kickoff back to our 40-yard line, we once again ran three unsuccessful plays and had to punt to them again. This time they took over on their own 9-yard line.

Again Ranum kept us off balance and ripped us for six and seven yards a pop. They were once again marching down the field. When they reached our 17-yard line I called a timeout to talk things over. Dan met the players as they came to the sideline and tried to encourage them to play harder and smarter. "Stay at home and read your keys!" he yelled.

As I listened to Dan, I remember having this very satisfied feeling thinking how smart I was to predict that the 4-4 was not the best way to stop our opponent. I felt good about the fact that in all the arguing over what defense to run, I was right and my assistants were wrong. *That's why I am the head coach,* I thought smugly.

Then it hit me. What was I so happy about? Here I was, about to lose the biggest game of my career and I felt smug about being correct in knowing which defense we should run.

At halftime, I took over the huddle and told the players that we were going to play our 60-front defense. I wanted to get penetration into the opposition's backfield before they could get started running north and south against us. Like a good soldier, Dan backed off. When our players returned to the field I told Dan, "Blitz the shit out of them! If we're going to stop them we need to do it from our 60 defense and disrupt things in the backfield."

Ranum fumbled on their next offensive play as our line slanted towards their wing back and knocked the ball free from the quarterback. During the fourth quarter, my eyes met Dan's. He flashed me a smile and gave two little nods of his head in recognition of the strategic change in our defense and the likely success it would bring.

* * *

Injuries and Intuition
– Timing Is Everything –

Bill Schoepflin was our best player and the *1976 Colorado High School Player-of-the-Year*. He was one of the best competitors I have ever coached in my 38 years and was not only a great athlete but also a dependable and responsible individual. I truly considered him to be the ideal "All-American Boy" - smart, athletic, honest, handsome, and tougher than nails. In other words, Bill was the best of the best. I would rank him right at the top despite the fact that he wasn't very big (5'10", 175-180 pounds) and he wasn't very fast (4.75 in the 40-yard dash). When it came to competing, he had a super attitude. Unfortunately, Bill separated his shoulder in our semi-final victory the week before the big Ranum game. Naturally, we would be a lesser team without him.

With Bill playing, I was sure that we had a decent chance to beat Ranum. Even without him I thought we might still be able to win if we could slow down their high scoring offense. Bill played tailback on offense and was our free safety on defense. On defense he made us very good; we were the best in the state that year. He was a great tackler and always was around the ball. We would probably miss him more on the defensive side than on offense. Don't get me wrong - he was a very good tailback. Back then, we only threw the ball about nine times each game and he carried it 20 or 25 times, averaging over 100 yards per game.

After our semi-final game, the doctors advised Bill and his father that if they could brace his shoulder and if he could stand the pain, he might possibly be able to play in the championship game. Bill's dad, Bud Schoepflin, was a jock himself. While his son was in high school, Bud built a weight room in their home where they would work out together. Back then, I would guess that Bud was outlifting Bill. Bud was one of the state's best baseball umpires. He understood sports, playing with pain, and how important his son was to our team.

Before the Ranum game, I was informed that in order to play, Bill would need to wear a harness, even though his partially-separated shoulder was mending. That meant he would not be able to raise his arm past his elbow. The doctors also advised us not to use him on kicking teams or on defense. With this in mind, my plan was not to use him unless we desperately needed to. Even though he was an extraordinary leader and competitor, I thought his injury would be too much for even him to overcome. He did not practice all week and the difference was obvious. Bill was our leader on the field and everyone knew it. We only inserted a few new plays for this game, so if Bill played, he would be able to run 95 percent of our offense.

Bill wanted to play and his dad wanted him to play. All week he was a pain in the butt, trying to convince me he was okay. On the Friday evening before the big game, Mr. Schoepflin and Bill met with me to discuss his playing time. "How much do you plan on using him?" Bud asked.

"Not at all if I can help it," I replied.

"Coach, I am okay with that harness on. I can still carry the ball. I'll just put it under my left arm," Bill chimed in. "It will be okay, honest."

"Bill, this game is important and with your shoulder the way it is, I am not sure you will be able to help us as much as you would otherwise," I replied.

After about 20 minutes of this discussion, both Bill and his father left with frowns on their faces. My strategy was to prepare them for the worse case scenario, knowing that in reality, I would use him – sparingly – and only if necessary.

Game day was a beautiful November Saturday in Boulder, Colorado. The morning newspaper quoted me as saying I didn't think Bill would be able to play in the game and that I had confidence in our backup tailback performing well for us. Yes, Bill would be suited out, but limited in his play, if at all.

We received the opening kickoff and on our first series of downs we went three-and-out, having to punt from our own 42-yard line. Our backup tailback was not able to find any running room on two of our first three plays. Ranum's defense was tougher than I had imagined.

Ranum scored on their first possession. We took the ensuing kickoff and once again were unable to gain a first down. The offense looked like they were playing in mud. Once again, we were forced to punt to our opponents. During Ranum's next drive, Bill came up to me on the sideline and shouted that he wanted to play. "Coach, put me in, my shoulder feels fine. If you want, I will take this damn harness off."

I looked at him and saw a determination I had never witnessed before. I knew he wanted to play and, of course, I wanted him to play. Bill was our leader on the field and everyone knew it - including me. "Okay," I told him. "The next time we have the ball I want you to go into the game."

Ranum finally made a mistake and fumbled the football deep in our territory. We were sending our offense out onto the field when I grabbed Bill by his game jersey. I told him to wait before he went into the game. A rage came over him. "Just wait a minute!" I yelled. "You're gonna play, but I want the offense to huddle up before you go in."

I knew that putting Bill into the game would energize our players and hopefully our fans. However, I wasn't sure anyone would notice him running out onto the field if he were clustered with 10 other players. So, to gain maximum impact from his insertion into the game, I held him back until the other players got into a huddle then I called a timeout. With our backup tailback still in the game and Bill standing anxiously by my side, I could see the confusion as the official signaled a timeout by Arvada.

After 10 seconds had elapsed, I looked at Bill, smiled, and winked at him. He got the message and smiled back, "We're going to win this game," I said as I released him to go into the game.

As Bill trotted onto the field, I felt a sensation I have never felt before or since. Our crowd went wild. The roar was tremendous. Even though we were in a large stadium, the ovation and excitement were awesome. I got goose bumps as Bill started waving his one good arm over his head as he approached the huddle. His teammates ran over to greet him before he got half-way on the field. Even his tailback replacement came sprinting off the field waving his arms and jumping as though a large burden had been lifted from his back. I knew we were ready to go.

On the first play, I called a sprint draw and Bill carried the ball for eight yards. Once again the roar from the crowd was electric. Our players sprinted back to the huddle as if they were Energizer bunnies. The game was on! Bill's presence in the game allowed his teammates to feel like they were complete and ready to win.

* * *

Transitioning to College

– Dreams and Disappointments –

During the 1978 season, Bill led the Arvada Redskins high school football team to the Colorado state championship. His talent and leadership were very instrumental in much of our success that season.

As a youngster, Bill's dream was always to play football for the University of Colorado Buffaloes. His strong family ties and great love of the state of Colorado made it a natural that he would want to stay in his home state and play on the most prestigious collegiate team. As an alumnus, I was all for him being a "Buff" as well.

During his junior season, Bill got inquiries from many colleges throughout the country. However, he did not fall into the recruiting frenzy, unlike most other high school players. Lavish trips and pampering by college coaches was not his cup of tea. He just wanted to play college football and dreamed of doing that in Boulder, Colorado.

In his senior year, Colorado informed Bill that they were not going to offer him a scholarship; instead, they would invite him to join as a "walk-on" and try to earn a scholarship. Bill and I both were devastated. Here was the best high school player I had ever coached and he couldn't get a scholarship to my own alma mater.

I called Steve Sidwell, CU's linebacker coach who was recruiting Bill at the time. Since Sidwell and I had played linebacker together at Colorado, I thought I might have a chance to convince him to reconsider his decision. I told him that just because Bill didn't run the 40 yard dash any better than 4.7 seconds, he had something inside him that made him a winner. "Sid," I said, "this kid is special. He has something inside him that makes him a winner. I don't think you guys could go wrong taking him."

"Listen, Bob," Sidwell replied, "I know he is a great kid, but after he met with Coach Crowder we decided not to offer him a scholarship position." He went on to explain Crowder's feeling, namely, "We can't win the Big Eight with 150 pound guys who run 4.7 seconds in the 40-yard dash."

Crowder apparently overlooked the fact that Bill was also a very good wrestler and had sucked his weight down to 150 pounds to make himself more competitive. This allowed him to wrestle in the lower weight class, whereas his normal football-playing weight was 175 to 180 pounds.

Despite my best efforts, the decision was final. Bill would not have a scholarship offer from the Buffaloes. We were both disappointed but turned to what we thought was the next best offer on the table.

Charlie Armey, recruiter for Colorado State University in Fort Collins, offered Bill a verbal scholarship to play for the CSU Rams. A "verbal scholarship" means that the school has decided to give a player a scholarship, but he cannot officially sign that scholarship agreement until the actual NCAA signing date—which was February 15 that year. Since Bill had been selected *First Team All-State* and chosen *Player-of-the-Year* in Colorado, CSU knew this would be huge for recruiting class rankings, if they could sign the best player in their own state.

Bill, his father, Bud, and I met to plan his next step in the recruiting process. Many schools, including Brigham Young University, New Mexico University, Northern Iowa, San Diego State University, etc., had shown high interest in signing Bill to a scholarship.

Most of these schools wanted him to visit their campuses; however, he had very little time to do so since he was in the middle of wrestling season. And of course, CSU already had a verbal commitment on the table.

One evening in December, we talked about distance from home, academics, football programs, coaches, styles of play and many other variables that contribute to helping a student athlete choose the most appropriate college. "Bill, tell me where you think you might want to go to (a) get your education, and (b) play football," I asked.

"Coach, I wanted to play for University of Colorado, but since they aren't interested in giving me a scholarship, I think I'll just accept the offer from Colorado State."

I asked for his reasoning.

He said, "I am not crazy about leaving the state, so playing for CSU in the Western Athletic Conference seems to be my next best option. I think I'll take their verbal commitment and just end it now. I don't have time to visit other schools and playing for the Rams means my family and friends can continue to watch me play."

Bud Schoepflin seemed satisfied with his son's decision; nevertheless, he asked me to explain in greater detail what was meant by the verbal commitment between Bill and CSU.

"A verbal means that the school and the athlete have verbally committed to sign the NCAA scholarship on the national signing date," I replied. "Both parties have entered into a verbal agreement, but the agreement is not legally binding until they both sign the scholarship document on February 15."

"What if Bill changes his mind between now and February 15?" Bud asked.

"Dad, I am not going to change my mind!" Bill cut in. "They want me and I want to go there. This is my second choice but I am excited about it."

I assured Mr. Schoepflin that Bill could change his mind. "Until he signs the actual scholarship papers," I said, "he can change his mind without any penalties."

"What if CSU changes its mind?" Bud inquired.

"They are not bound to sign him, just as he is not bound to sign with them. It is a verbal agreement by both parties and each party can change its mind," I said. "If Bill is sure CSU is where he wants to go, then he should verbally commit and end the recruiting process now. He can concentrate on wrestling and be assured that he still has his scholarship. I have never heard of a school reneging on a verbal offer unless the athlete gets hurt or does something illegal or dumb. That would sour any school, at any time. If Bill is sure this is what he wants to do than I recommend he verbally commit and end the process now."

After another day of thinking about his future, Bill came to school and told me he definitely wanted to commit to CSU and get out of the recruiting process. We then called CSU and told them if the verbal commitment was still available, Bill would like to verbally commit. Everyone seemed happy.

I now had the obligation to call all the schools that were still interested in recruiting Bill to tell them he had verbally committed to CSU and that he did not want to consider them further. This was good for Bill. It meant that he would not have to answer the numerous phone calls he received each night from coaches still trying to convince him to attend their schools.

Bud was pleased. I was happy. Bill finally felt free to concentrate solely on winning the state wrestling championship without having to worry about where he might attend school next year. Everything seemed fine and dandy.

Until February 12, that is. Three days before the February 15 signing date, Bill came into my office. He had a dour look on his face. I could tell something was wrong. "What's up, Bill?" I asked.

"Coach, CSU called last night and told me that they couldn't honor my scholarship," he stated softly.

"What?" I yelled. "What do you mean they can't honor their commitment to you?"

"Coach Armey called me last night. He said they over-committed on verbals and had to cut back in order to stay under the NCAA allowance. He said I was one of the players they decided to cut. He told me I could walk-on, and maybe they might have something for me after my freshman year."

"That's bullshit!" I stormed. "They can't do that. I never heard of such a thing. Let me call up there and see what the hell is going on."

Sark Arsalian was head coach at CSU. I picked up the phone and immediately called his office. His secretary said he wasn't in.

"Ask Coach Arsalian to call me back ASAP," I told her. "It is very important that I talk to him today."

Bill went on to class while I sat by the phone to await a call-back from Arsalian. It never came. About an hour later Coach Armey called.

"Charlie, what the hell is going on?" I asked. "Schoepflin tells me that you guys have reneged on your verbal and now you want him to come as a walk-on."

Charlie affirmed that they had over-committed on verbals. Since CSU really didn't need any more defensive backs in their freshmen class, they had to rescind their previous offer to Bill.

"That's not right Charlie," I protested. "Here it is, three days before signing date and you guys want to pull out? That's bullshit and you know it!"

"Bob, we met last night as a staff and made the final decision," he replied. "I am sorry, but we have to do what we think is best for the program. Bill is a good enough athlete that he will probably earn a scholarship very quickly when he joins our program."

"Charlie, I personally counseled that kid and told his family that he had a scholarship to CSU. We canceled all other visits and kept other schools from recruiting him—all because of your verbal commitment to sign him on the 15th. And now, a few days before signing date and the best high school player I have ever coached is sitting without a football scholarship. That's not right."

We exchanged a few choice words and then I slammed down the phone, disgusted and distressed. I called the NCAA and pleaded our case to them. The NCAA seemed interested and promised to look into the situation, but they couldn't offer much real encouragement since verbal commitments are not binding on either party.

I talked with a couple other high school coaches that evening. I learned that ours was not an isolated case. CSU had, in fact, done the same thing to two other high school players in the state.

It was apparent that CSU verbally committed to more players than they could legally sign. They counted on attrition to get them below the legal limit. When that strategy failed, they tried to convince some of the verbals to be walk-ons and earn scholarships. Apparently, this was not the first time that CSU had pulled this stunt. Though the practice was not illegal, in my judgment it was certainly unethical.

I would not stand for that. I met with Ron Mitchell, our athletic director and Jack Jost, the school principal. After I recounted the story, we all decided that the appropriate action would be for Arvada to blackball CSU football coaches from recruiting on our campus in the future.

The next day, I wrote a letter to the president and athletic director of Colorado State University. I explained the situation that occurred with regard to Schoepflin. The letter concluded by telling them that since Arvada could not condone CSU's recruiting tactics, none of CSU's football coaches would be allowed in the school to talk to our players. I sent copies to Coaches Armey and Arsalian.

Not long afterwards, a sports reporter with a local newspaper called and wanted to know where some of my players had accepted scholarship offers. She specifically wanted information about Bill Schoepflin since our team had won the state championship that year and Bill was voted *Player-of-the-Year* in Colorado.

She was flabbergasted when I told her the story about Bill and CSU. Knowing that Bill was the *Player-of-the-Year* and yet had no scholarship offer was a real scoop for her. I told her that as a result of this, we would not allow CSU to come on our campus and recruit our football players.

Somehow she got the story wrong. The next morning's sports headlines trumpeted: **CSU Blackballed from Jefferson County.** There were 12 schools in the Jefferson County School District, one of the largest school districts in the U.S. The recruiting ban applied to just one—Arvada. The article was incorrect.

* * *

Postscript

Arvada won the state championship game against Ranum, 12-7, and Dan Patterson eventually went on to become a very successful head coach. Even though Bill Schoepflin did not have one of his more stellar performances that day, I am sure that his presence on the field made the critical difference.

Fortunately for Bill, a few days after the national signing date during his senior year, BYU had a scholarship still available that they offered to Bill. He accepted.

BYU and CSU were in the Western Athletic Conference and played each other yearly. BYU never lost to CSU while Bill was a member of the team. Bill Schoepflin was a starter for BYU going to four Bowl games and making a big play in the 1982 Fiesta Bowl – a play that was instrumental in BYU's victory that year.

* * *

Persistence Pays Off
– Sixty Free Throws Make a Difference –

Of all the good athletes I've had the privilege of coaching over the years, the most determined and intensely competitive was a young girl named Mary Gillach. In 1976, she was a sophomore at Arvada and quite unexpectedly, I was given the opportunity to be her coach – in basketball, that is.

Arvada High School was in the largest classification in the state and sports were a very integral part of the program. We had an exceptionally good football team that year and half-way through the season, I thought we had an excellent chance to win the state championship – which we eventually did.

Jack Jost, our principal, was a real go-getter. He wanted Arvada not only to excel in academics but also to stand out in the performing arts and athletics. He called me into his office during the middle of football season. "Bob, I need a big favor," he said.

"What do you need, Boss?" I asked.

He told me the girls' basketball coach had resigned due to health problems, putting the program in jeopardy, since the start of the season was just a month away. "You're the only one on the entire staff who has any basketball coaching experience," Jost explained.

As a matter of fact, I had indeed coached the junior varsity team at Saint Joseph High School in Denver. However, this occurred early in my coaching career and it was a boys' team. I had never coached a girls' team. When your boss requests your help to bail him out of a difficult situation, you usually try to comply. And an extra $1,000 in my paycheck was a nice incentive.

The girls had a good team returning from the year before. Members included Laura Bott, Bobbie Brown, and Coleen Manning - three good players. These girls were dedicated to the team, and during the off-season they practiced many hours to make themselves even better. A 5'3" sophomore girl named Mary Gillach provided the additional spark this team needed.

Mary was a real "gym rat." Her father coached basketball at a different school, so she spent many, many hours in the gym. She had a sweet little 10-15 foot jumper, shot 61 percent from the free throw line and could dribble the ball with the best of them. She was dribbling between her legs and behind her back even before it became vogue. It was very hard to take the ball away from her because she was as quick as a water bug and could dribble with either hand. If teams pressed, we wanted to get the ball to her. She was our press breaker and a strong addition to the team.

With the end of football season, I turned full attention to coaching these girls. I pushed them as hard as I did my football players. Conditioning was a focus early in the season and I ran them ragged. I yelled at them as we went through their drills just as I did with my football team, the difference being that I didn't cuss at them - at least not as much. Also, I never slapped the girls on the butt as coaches tend to do with male players. I learned to pat them, in a fatherly way, on their shoulders instead.

Another thing I had to get used to was when and when not to be, in their locker room. Jokingly I would always bang on the locker room door before entering, and yell, "MAN IN THE LOCKER ROOM! EVERYONE CLOSE YOUR EYES!"

We won 18 games that season, but with the talent we had, we

should have won even more. Who said coaching doesn't matter?

One of my coaching techniques in both football and basketball was to have an exit interview with each player after the season concluded. I met with each girl individually for about 45 minutes. With the seniors, I would talk to them about their futures and how they evaluated their team experience that season. I would ask what they like and disliked and what we could do to improve the program. With returning players, we would talk about goals and off-season programs. I would tell them what skills I believed they needed to improve their game.

Mary was the first one to sign up for an interview. She was bold and aggressive, just as she was on the basketball court. After a few minutes of small talk, Mary asked, "Coach, what do I need to do to be a better player?" Only a sophomore, but she was already taking control of my meeting.

"Well, Mary," I said, overcoming my surprise at her forcefulness, "since you only shot 61 percent from the free throw line, I would hope you can improve on that percentage next season." Since she was our ball handler, our opponents naturally put her on the charity line quite often. I reasoned that a higher free-throw percentage from her would mean a higher point total and possibly more victories for us.

Before I could get any other words out of my mouth, Mary interrupted to ask, "Okay, what percent do you think I should shoot for next season?" We talked about it for a little while and both agreed she should shoot at least 71 percent from the free throw line next season.

"Coach, what do I need to do to reach that mark?" she asked.

I told her I thought if she shot 60 free throws every day from now until the start of the season, she would probably improve that much. After talking about summer camps and other things, an enthusiastic Mary bounced out of the meeting.

Three days after spring break, I got a phone call from Mary's mother. "Coach, I need your help. Our family drove to Iowa for vacation and every day we were on the road, Mary made us stop in various towns along the way to find a place where she could shoot her damned 60 throws. We had to find parks that had baskets. Have you ever been in strange community and tried to find an outdoor basket? Not fun! There was one town where we couldn't find any public place for her to shoot, but we found a basket in someone's driveway and I had to knock on some stranger's door to ask if Mary could shoot her 60 free throws. This is getting out of hand. Is this really what you advised?" I assured her that it was.

On a snowy Sunday two weeks later, I needed to go to my office at school to catch up on some paperwork. Colorado was having one of its typical late spring snow storms and the temperature was terribly cold. Arvada High School was a big school and quite expectedly was locked and empty on a Sunday. As I entered the darkened building and walked toward my office right outside the large gymnasium, I heard a noise.

Ordinarily the gym lights were turned off when the facility was not in use; however, there were two little incandescent night lights that always remained lit above each basket. Even so, they didn't provide enough light for me to see well in the gloom of this large gymnasium.

Hearing the noise spooked me and I thought I had better call the police because it sounded like someone else was also in the area. I thought possibly I had surprised a burglar. "Hey, who's in here?" I shouted in my loudest and most stern voice. I was greeted with nothing but silence. Again I called out, "Who's here?" Again no response. "Okay, I am going to call the police," I threatened as I started towards my office.

Finally I heard a faint, soft voice. "It's me, Coach Cortese."

"Who is 'me'?" I responded, feeling braver about the situation now since at least the person knew who I was.

"Mary," came the reply.

"Mary? What are you doing here and how in the world did you get in the building?" I asked as I started towards the direction of her voice.

As I approached her, I could see she had on boots, gloves, a parka, and a black knit cap. She also had a basketball.

"Mary, what in the world are you doing here?" I repeated.

"Shooting my 60 free throws."

"Mary, are you crazy?" I asked. "You can't be in here when the school is closed. Besides, how did you get in the building in the first place?"

There was a long pause, and then this pretty little athlete started bouncing the basketball she had tucked under her arm.

"Mary?" I questioned, this time more forcefully.

She explained that she had shimmied up the gutter on the side of the vocational building, crossed over the flat roof, and then shimmied down the gutter into a courtyard in the center of the school. From there, she went over to a basement window that led into the girls' locker room. A window had been left unlocked. Finally, Mary had climbed down into the locker room and entered the gym. She assured me that she did not harm anything; all she wanted to do was shoot baskets when the weather was too cold outside.

"Coach," she said, "you told me I had to shoot 60 free throws every day until next season starts and that is exactly what I am trying to do."

"Well, is it working?" I asked.

"Watch," she said, "I'll make at least eight out of 10." It was amazing to watch this scrappy little female shoot her free throws in a nocturnal environment. If we ever played in an unlit gym, Mary would have excelled. Nevertheless, she expressed sharp disappointment in herself for only making seven out of 10.

* * *

Postscript

Following the next football season, I took a job coaching at the University of Colorado, which meant the girls' basketball program had to find another new coach. Despite coaching changes, Mary continued to excel and shot 73 percent from the free throw line that year and almost 80 percent her senior year. She enrolled at the University of Northern Colorado. During her 1983 senior year, Mary won the NCAA Division II doubles tennis championship with her teammate, Sandra Elliott. With two master's degrees, she is currently a highly successful real estate broker in the Boston area.

* * *

The Case of the Missing Equipment Manager
– Popcorn Anyone? –

Walking through the halls of Arvada High School, I often scouted prospects who could serve as my team's equipment manager. I always tried to fill these positions with students from different backgrounds and I thought that the more people you got involved in your football program, the better chance for success. I already had three student managers, but felt that we were still lacking something.

As I walked passed the special education class, a young man called out and tried to get my attention.

"Coach Cortese, Coach Cortese," he shouted.

"Yes?" I answered.

"Sorry about that, Bob," said Janet Holloway, the school's special education teacher. "Fred, behave yourself."

"It's okay," I said. "What did he want?"

Janet quietly stepped out into the hall and closed the door behind her. "He wants to be on the football team," she said.

"Really?" I responded.

"Normally he's a quiet, well-behaved kid. But I have to keep the door closed on Friday afternoons," she said.

"Why is that?" I asked.

"He gets so excited when the football players troop past my room wearing their jerseys. I think Fred's your biggest fan," Janet glanced at her watch. "Well, I should get back to work. We have a lot of things to cover today," she said.

I walked back to my class, not giving Fred another thought. At practice after school that day, I had our team going through 7-on-7 drills when I noticed Fred sitting outside his mother's car watching from a distance.

"Take over for a minute, Dennis," I said to my defensive coordinator, Dennis Jost. "I think I've found our new equipment manager."

I made my way down the road to the parking lot to discuss things with Fred. "Fred, how would you like to be a member of my team?" I asked.

"Well, I would like that a lot, Coach," he said, smiling from ear-to-ear. "But you will probably have to talk to my mom first."

Fred's mom was standing nearby and listened patiently to my spiel.

"Coach Cortese, I appreciate the offer," she said, "but I am not sure it would be in Fred's best interest for him to play football," she said. She took me by the arm and guided me away from Fred. "He would love to be a member of the team. Nobody loves Arvada High School football more than Fred, but unfortunately he just does not have the mental capability to play organized sports."

"He doesn't have to play football to be a member of the team,"

I explained. "Actually, I'm looking for an equipment manager and I thought your son would be great for the job." She hesitated, but then agreed to let Fred give it a try.

Since our goal was to help Fred be successful, we gave him appropriate jobs that he was well capable of performing. His responsibilities included filling the water bottles and bringing them onto the field for the players during time outs. We also gave him the task of keeping the kick off tee and the extra-point tee in his possession at all times. As primary keeper of the tees, he was responsible for getting the tee to the kicker before each field goal and extra point. He would retrieve it after the play. We even had a little carrying pouch made for him so he could keep track of the tees and have them available as needed. Fred did a great job and it was obvious that he was really enjoying himself.

It was mid-October and we were set to take on our biggest rival of the season, Arvada West. Most schools play their rivals in the first three weeks of the season and since AWHS was also in our conference, it added to the intensity of the rivalry. As game time approached, the air was electric. There's nothing like Friday nights in high school football; there is just something magical about them.

We won the toss and chose to kick off to start the game. Fred was his usual self, sprinting to Brett McKnight, our kicker at the time, to deliver the tee. "Here you go, Brett," Fred said.

"Thanks, man," Brett replied.

We dug ourselves into a hole early, trailing 14-0 at the end of the first quarter. Finally we started moving the ball in the second quarter. With a little over five minutes left in the quarter, we scored a touchdown.

Fred gave the place kicker the tee for the point-after try and pulled out the kickoff tee even before the ball was snapped for the PAT. He rushed onto the field and gave the tee to Brett. Fred was so good at his new responsibilities that we didn't even look for him before PATs. His actions were accurate and automatic.

We trailed 14-7 when one of our defensive backs, Mike Brown, picked off a pass and returned it 20 yards for a touchdown. After a brief huddle, the place kicker and the team ran onto the field. Brett got all the way to the 15-yard line before he realized that he did not have the tee. It was such a crucial moment in the game - our chance to tie the score.

"Where is Fred?" Brett yelled to the sideline. "I don't have the tee to kick the ball. Where the hell is Fred?"

Everyone on the sideline began calling for Fred. Fred was no-where to be found. Not only was there no Fred, there was also no extra-point tee to be found.

Meanwhile, the play clock was winding down and we were about to be assessed a penalty. Over 5,000 fans sat in the stands oblivious to what was actually going on.

"Coach Cortese, what in the hell are you doing?" one of the fans screamed.

I called a timeout and after a short time spent looking up and down the players' box for Fred, I quickly yelled for the offense to run out onto the field and go for two. There was no way we could kick the extra point without the tee. This added to the fan's confusion since it was still only the second quarter.

"He's lost it," I overheard our team doctor who was standing next to the bench, say. "He's clearly out of his mind. Why would he do that, when Brett hasn't missed a kick all year?"

Luckily my quarterback was able to take it in from three yards out to get the two points. That gave us a 15-14 lead to carry into the locker room at half-time.

As the players were coming off the field after the two-point at-tempt, I spotted Fred walking back into the players' box clutching the pouch which I knew contained the elusive tees. He was holding a large bag of popcorn in his other hand.

"Fred, where were you?" I yelled. "We needed the tees; we just scored a touchdown!"

Fred calmly looked at me clearly thinking I had just asked a real dumb-ass question. "You know, Coach," he said, "I didn't get to eat much dinner tonight. That popcorn smelled so good that it made me hungry so I went and got something to eat before the halftime lines at the concession stands got too long."

What could I say?

* * *

Postscript

It was a hard-fought game with a final score of 15-14. Fred's appetite turned out to be the game-winner for us.

9

Jump-Start in the Desert
— What Happens in Silver City Stays in Silver City —

I did not look with favor on the prospect of my players traveling 14 hours by bus - almost 700 miles - to play a football game. But that was our normal mode of travel at Mesa State College, where I was head football coach back in 1986. We simply didn't have the budget to fly "big time" as did the top tier, better-funded and more prestigious football powerhouses.

Our destination was Silver City, New Mexico, home of the Mustangs of Western New Mexico University. Western New Mexico University was tucked down in the far southwest corner of the state, just 80 miles from the Mexican border and 45 miles from Arizona.

Due to the unreasonable driving distance, we chartered a 50-seat airplane from some charter company two weeks before the actual game. We decided that we would fly to Silver City on the day of the game, play the game, and fly back to Grand Junction right afterwards. We would offset some of the extra expense by cutting out two days of travel. The flight would take about two to three hours.

One big problem we had flying into Silver City was that there was no airport big enough to handle the landing of a 50-seat airplane. However, just 14 miles outside the city limits was an old runway used by the air force to practice taking off and landing bigger planes. It was closed down at the time. All it had was a runway, nothing else. No buildings, parking lot or control tower. Just a runway out in the middle of the country.

It was a very hot September day. The sun was pounding down and the temperature at kickoff was in the high 90s. The Mustangs were tough and battled us right down to the wire. It was a hard-fought game but we won 30-24. Following the game, we happily consumed cheeseburgers, french fries, and cold drinks which were delivered to the locker room. The players showered, ate, and boarded the bus headed back to the abandoned airstrip where the plane was waiting. We all were tired, sore, and hot from the battle of the game.

When we reached the plane on the runway, one of our very young-looking pilots announced that since the load on the plane was so heavy, we would have to wait until the sun went down behind the mountain pass just to the west of us, before we could actually take off. He said that when the sun was behind the mountains, the temperatures cooled off and the plane could then get more lift due to the cooler air. I gulped thinking about the extra weight I fudged on, in trying to get everything and everybody aboard.

Since we were out in the country surrounded by nothing but a small farm off in the distance, the players had to sit out on the ground and wait for the cooler dusk air. There was no way they could tolerate the heat inside the plane and the bus had already departed. The plane had been turned off since we landed some nine hours earlier, so the temperature inside was unbearable.

What a sight! Fifty players and numerous coaches sitting out on the concrete runway with nothing to do. The sun was still pounding down on us and the players were bitching about when they could board the plane and get cooled off.

Finally, the sun settled behind the mountain and the pilots thought they could now get enough lift to clear the mountain. We all boarded the plane for our trip home.

Since we had paid for the charter, I thought it would be a good experience for me to see how the pilots started the plane and prepared for takeoff. I asked them if it would be okay for me to stand behind them in the cockpit as they went through their pre-flight routine. Now remember, this was pre-9/11. They said that would be okay, but as soon as the plane started to move I would have to go back to my seat and buckle up. Fine with me.

Since the plane hadn't been started yet, the temperature inside was still well over 100 degrees. It actually felt like a sauna. The players were happy with the strong victory and no doubt felt justified in complaining about the heat and their need of some cooler air. Victories seemed to energize and empower them both on and off the field. If we had lost the game not one person would have complained about the heat, because they knew how upset I would have been. I could be pretty hard when I am upset and if we had lost, I would have been very upset.

I watched as the pilot asked the co-pilot to open the book and start reading the checklist to him. This kind of bothered me because I assumed these guys had flown enough that they didn't need the checklist book. But what did I know?

The co-pilot said, "First check whatever."

"Check," said the pilot.

"Second check whatever."

"Check," said the pilot.

"Third check whatever."

"Check," said the pilot.

"Fourth check whatever."

"Check," said the pilot.

"Fifth check, turn the key and start," directed the co-pilot. The pilot turned the key and nothing happened. They looked at each other with blank stares. After about 10 seconds, the pilot told the co-pilot to close the book and reopen it to start the plane.

The co-pilot said, "First check whatever."

"Check," said the pilot.

"Second check whatever."

"Check," said the pilot.

"Third check whatever."

"Check," said the pilot.

"Fourth check whatever."

"Check," said the pilot.

"Fifth check, turn the key and start," directed the co-pilot. Once again the pilot turned the key and still nothing happened.

Now I was beginning to wonder what in the hell was going on.

"Let's try it again," said the pilot. "Close the book and let's start again."

"Check," said the co-pilot. He closed the book and then opened it again to the first page.

The co-pilot once again said, "First check whatever."

"Check," said the pilot.

"Second check whatever."

"Check," said the pilot.

"Third check whatever."

"Check," said the pilot.

"Fourth check whatever."

"Check," said the pilot.

"Fifth check, turn the key and start," directed the co-pilot. For the third time, the pilot turned the key and for the third time, nothing happened.

Naturally I was really wondering what these two guys were doing. I considered the possibility that maybe we had two pilots who didn't know how to start a plane, much less fly it. The pilots ran through the whole procedure once again, including closing the book and starting from scratch. When the plane still did not start, the pilot looked confused. He turned to me and said, "Coach, we can't get it started." He told me they were going to radio back to their home office (location unknown) for suggestions.

Since my players were understandably hot and restless, we decided to let them off the plane again so they could cool off while the pilots tried to figure out what needed to be done. Since this was in the early 80s, cell phone assistance was not an option.

We finally got all the players and coaches back off the plane and onto the runway again. By now it was dark and the temperature had dropped considerably. The players finally seemed more comfortable, but were still upset that we weren't on our way home.

The two pilots finally got off the plane and told me that one of them was going to walk to the farm house in the distance, probably about two miles away, and ask to use the phone.

A half hour later the pilot came back, riding in a rusted-out 1955 Chevy truck that reminded me of the one used in the old TV series, "The Beverly Hillbillies," or perhaps a relic from some past war. It belonged to the farmer who lived nearby.

The pilot told me to get everyone back on the plane because he would soon fix the problem and we would be on our way. I did as he requested, but reminded him how hot it was on the plane saying that I wasn't really sure just how long I could keep the players from revolting.

When I asked him what he was going to do to resolve our ignition problem, he replied that he was going to jump-start the plane's battery by using the farmer's jumper cables hooked up to the old truck. That would get the engine to turn over and we could then begin our flight home.

I was shocked, to say the least. "What in hell are you talking about?" I asked.

The pilot calmly responded that since our battery was dead, all we needed was to get it jump-started and then we would be fine - once the engines were running.

Holy cow! I thought. *Not only are they going to jump-start this plane, but they are planning to get the power from a truck that I wouldn't be caught dead driving in for more than a 100 yards!*

I knew the players and coaches would be scared to death if they thought these two young pilots were going to jump-start the plane using the power from the old truck. I told the pilots not to do anything until I had all the players and coaches back inside the plane so they wouldn't see how we were going to get power.

"Everyone back on the plane!" I ordered. "These guys got the problem figured out and we are close to taking off."

It was amazing to see how much power coaches have over their players. They all scrambled aboard again, but probably only because I was their coach and ordered them to do so.

I stayed with the pilot, who got the jumper cables from the truck. The co-pilot hooked up the cables to the battery and then told the pilot, who had now gone into the cockpit, to turn the key. Twenty seconds or so later, the engines were purring like kittens.

We gave 20 dollars to the farmer, jumped back on the plane, closed the door behind us, and started back to Grand Junction.

I held my breath as we taxied down the runway and said a silent prayer that we had enough lift to get over that damned mountain. I knew the players sweated off some poundage during the hot game, but I was unsure about all those cheeseburgers we let them devour before the trip back to the airplane.

* * *

Postscript

The trip back home was uneventful. The players and coaches slept like babies. I breathed a sigh of relief and silently resolved that what they didn't know could never hurt them. Mutiny can be an awful thing.

10

Dealing with Death

– 275 Pounds of Grief –

One of the hardest things a coach ever has to do is also one of the most personally rewarding, and that is helping a young person cope with the harsh realities of life. And probably no reality is harder to cope with than the death of a parent. Telling a player that his parent is gone forever means telling him he has lost the parental love and attention that was given uniquely to him. Nothing ever feels right when a parent dies. When a college student loses a parent, it is somewhat like a child losing one. In most cases, a college student has only been away from home for a relatively short period of time and still feels much more connected to his home life than to his new life within his college community.

Twice in my coaching career I was the one called on to inform a team member of the death of one of his parents. My memories are still vivid. Over the years, it was my responsibility to share such devastating news with two of my players: Eddie Ford and Bill Walker. It was the toughest duty imaginable.

The first time occurred while I was coaching running backs at the University of Colorado. I was at the chalk board going over our different pass protections with all the fullbacks and tailbacks when

Coach Bill Mallory came into the meeting room. I knew something was up because Coach Bill never interrupted our sacred meeting times.

"Bob, I need to talk to you out in the hall," he said. I put down the chalk and walked with him outside the meeting room. *I hope I'm not in trouble,* I remember thinking.

Coach Mallory was a strong, disciplined man but it was obvious that something was bothering him. Family was an important part of his life. He built his football teams around the premise: *WE ARE FAMILY.*

"What's up Coach," I asked?

"Eddie Ford's father just passed away," Coach Mallory stated with tears welling in his eyes.

"Oh shit!" I exclaimed. "How and when did it happen?"

I don't actually remember all the details about Mr. Ford's death but I do remember that Eddie was very close to his father.

We were always careful to keep an eye on all of our players but our freshmen got even more off-field attention. Eddie was no exception. He was a freshman fullback from San Diego and a very good player with a bright future; we sure didn't want him to return to California because he was homesick. Accordingly, Coach Mallory insisted that we give him special attention as he weaned himself from home.

Coach Mallory told me that Eddie's family had called and requested that he be sent home immediately. "So you pull him out of the meeting and tell him," Coach said, "and I'll take care of his travel arrangements."

I was stunned that Coach Mallory wanted me to break the news. "Don't you think it would be better if you tell him?" I asked tentatively. Since I really didn't want to be the one to break the news to this young man, I hoped that Coach would reconsider his role and be the messenger himself. No response. "I can make all the travel arrangements to get him home ASAP," I suggested hopefully.

Coach Mallory considered my suggestion for what seemed like an eternity, head turned away, and eyes clouded with tears. Then, as if closing the cover of his notebook, he abruptly turned toward me and said, "You tell him!" and walked away. He paused at the door, looked back at me still standing there, and said, "You have a good relationship with him."

I have never known a tougher or more disciplined man than Coach Bill Mallory. As my mentor, he taught me not only about the game of football, but also about life and managing people. But death was obviously too tough for this strong and sensitive man to deal with.

I was still in shock, not only about Eddie's father's death, but also about how I was going to break the news to him. I had never done this before, had never seen it done, and never learned how to do it in "Coaching 101."

I spent a few moments to gather my thoughts, then returned to the meeting room and called Eddie into the hall. I told him we needed to find an empty room where we wouldn't be disturbed. He looked at me quizzically.

Once inside the room, I said, "Eddie, someone from your family called and told Coach Bill that your father died this morning."

"WHAT? Coach, don't play games like that," he replied as he rubbed his head. "That's not funny. Who called?"

Now my eyes started to well up. "It's true, Eddie. One of your family members called asking us to tell you that your dad passed away. They want you home as soon as possible. Coach Mallory is making travel arrangements for you now. I am really sorry, Eddie."

After a few minutes spent convincing him it was true, He yelled, "NOOOOO! Why are you doing this to me? Why? Why?

Where? How?" He was starting to grasp the magnitude of the message. He broke down, crying "Coach, tell me it's not true. Please, Coach, tell me it's not true!"

"I am sorry Eddie, it is true."

After what seemed like a long period of silence but in actuality was probably only a few seconds, Eddie started to scream again. "NO! NO! NO!" He then picked up a chair and threw it against the wall. Before I could intervene, he grabbed the table and turned it over. I froze, not knowing what to do. Finally, I rushed him, wrapped my arms around him and tried to hold him close to me. I knew Eddie was strong, but I had never felt such strength as I did trying to hold onto this raging, grieving bull.

Hearing the commotion, some of the other coaches rushed into the room to help stabilize the situation. After things quieted down, I went directly to my office and for some reason locked the door behind me. I'm still not sure why I did that. I sat at my desk, put my head between my arms, and I cried.

It hurts to see someone you work with on a daily basis go through such a sorrowful experience. Eddie Ford was not only a good football player, but he was also a wonderful young man. He did everything we asked him to do. He wanted to be a part of our football family and he was.

Sometimes after a parent of a college student dies, the student finds it difficult to return to school. However, since Eddie's father had made it clear that he wanted his son to get a college degree, Eddie did return to school.

Later that season, as a second team freshman fullback, Eddie Ford was a major force in helping us beat the University of Missouri in Columbia. Our starting All-Big Eight fullback, James Mayberry, got hurt in the first half, and Eddie was forced to play the entire second half. He rushed over, under and around the Tigers for 102 yards and scored two touchdowns. We won the game 28-26. In the locker room after the game he told me his dad would have been proud of how he played.

* * *

Bill Walker was the second team member who lost a parent while playing for me. It was the spring of 1993 and I was coaching at Fort Hays State University in Hays, Kansas. The call came early in the morning. Boy, did I hate those 3:30 a.m. phone calls. Nothing - I mean *nothing* good ever came from them. As a college football coach responsible for over 100 players, I knew that an early morning phone call generally meant someone was in trouble or something was drastically wrong.

The phone rang and I groaned to my wife that I was way too tired to answer the phone.

Just let it ring," I said. But after the seventh ring, I figured I ought to at least find out who was trying to reach me with such persistence. "Hello?" I answered, with what I hoped was an authorative tone.

"Hello, Coach Cortez?" a male voice questioned.

"Yes, this is Coach CorTESE," I replied, correcting the pronunciation of my last name. I wasn't always very patient with people at 3 a.m.

"Coach, my name is Larry Corson. I am Billy Walker's uncle. I have been trying to get in touch with Billy and can't find him." He paused to clear his throat. "His mother was in a car accident this afternoon."

"How serious?" I asked.

He paused again. "She died a couple of hours ago. I have been trying to get in touch with him to give him the bad news."

That got my attention. I sat up on the side of the bed as my wife looked at me worriedly. She knew something was wrong.

"I believe he lives in the dorm," I told Mr. Corson. "Wait and I will get you his phone number." I always kept a list at home of the addresses and phone numbers of all my players.

"No, we have his dorm number, but no one answers," Mr. Corson replied. "Do you think you can find him?"

"I don't know where he might be if he isn't in his room," I said. We talked briefly about the need to get Bill home as soon as possible. Mr. Corson gave me more details about the accident. I told him that I thought it was good that he hadn't reached Bill by phone because it had been my experience that receiving such terrible information over the phone could have devastating effects. I assured Bill's uncle that I would find him and let him know what had happened; and I would make sure Bill got in touch with his family.

The first person I called after I hung up with Mr. Corson was Bill Kralicek, my offensive line coach. Kralicek was Bill's position coach. Offensive line coaches and their players seem to have a genuinely strong bond. Kralicek could find out things from his players that I could never have learned on my own.

I hadn't finished dressing when Kralicek called back with the information on Bill's likely whereabouts. He said he learned that Bill was probably sleeping over at his girlfriend's apartment. She didn't live on campus, but his source gave him her local street address. Unfortunately, his source didn't have a phone number for her.

Coach Kralicek asked if I wanted him to find Bill and share the sad news. I considered his offer but remembered how I felt when Coach Bill Mallory gave me the unenviable job of telling Eddie Ford about the death of his father when I was an assistant coach.

"That's okay," I told Kralicek. "It's better I tell him myself. I believe it is the responsibility of the head coach." I could tell my loyal assistant was relieved that he didn't have to be the bearer of such tragic news.

While driving around the back streets of Hays, looking for the apartment, I mentally rehearsed how to break the news to Bill. I found myself replaying the earlier experience with Eddie Ford and this, in turn, helped me organize my thoughts for talking with Bill. Bill was much bigger than Eddie, but I didn't think any stronger. Standing 6'2" and weighing about 275 pounds, Bill would be easier to console and control, if necessary, if he were seated when I gave him the news.

After finally finding the correct address, I knocked on the door and got no response. Thirty seconds later, I pounded again, only this time loud enough to make sure I woke anyone sleeping inside. A light came on and shortly thereafter, a soft woman's voice asked timidly, "Who is it?"

"It's Coach Cortese and I am looking for Bill Walker. Is he here?"

After a long pause, the voice responded, "No, he's not here."

"It's very important that I talk to him. Do you know where he is?"

Another long pause. "No, I don't."

"He's not in any trouble," I said. "But I need to pass on some very important information to him, so if Bill's here, I really need to talk to him please."

After another long pause, I heard the door being unlocked. Standing half-covered behind the door, a pretty girl peeked out and asked, "What information?"

"I need to talk to Bill," I said. "Is he here?"

"Let him in." The voice sounded like that of Bill Walker.

As I entered and looked around the dimly lit room, I could see that, except for a small towel loosely-wrapped around her body, the girl appeared to have no clothes on. Bill Walker was standing in a doorway wearing shorts and nothing else.

"I need to talk to you, Bill," I said. Motioning towards a red bean-bag chair, I said, "Please, sit down here."

Bill was hesitant at first. Not knowing what to expect from this early morning meeting with his coach was very evident by the perplexed look on his face. But like all good athletes, he followed my instructions and sat down. That was good since the bean-bag chair was very low to the ground and therefore, it would be hard for him to get both into and out of, and therefore easier to constrain if necessary.

"What's up, Coach?" he asked.

"Bill, I hate to tell you this but your mother was killed yesterday in a car accident." I paused. "Your Uncle Larry has been trying to reach you. Since he has been unable to locate you, he called and told me about it a little while ago."

In the background, I could hear the girl scream, "Oh, my God!"

I stood over Bill, waiting for a reaction. Nothing. He sat there for about 30 seconds with a blank look on his face not saying a word.

Finally, reality set in. Bill started to realize the magnitude of what I had just told him, but I sensed he wasn't sure he believed it. "Coach, are you sure?" he asked. "Maybe someone was playing a trick on you. You know how guys are always fucking around."

"No, Bill, I am sure. When your uncle called, he gave me all the details."

Rage and sadness seemed to hit him simultaneously. He yelled, "FUCK!" He attempted to get up out of the bean-bag chair. Since I thought it would be in his best interest to stay seated, I put my hands on his shoulders and, with very little effort, restrained him.

"Just stay there, Bill!" I said, perhaps too loudly.

"No, let me up, God damn it," he shouted as he struggled with me to get to his feet. So much for following the directions of his coach.

"Stay down there." I once again pushed to keep him in the chair.

We wrestled with each other. "Shit, let me up," he hollered, equally loudly.

Suddenly, Bill's towel-attired girlfriend joined the fray by jumping on my back and hitting me, in an attempt to have me loosen my grip on Bill's shoulders. Most men probably wouldn't mind having a semi-naked young coed riding on his back, but given the situation, it was ridiculous. Her persistence, coupled with Bill's strength, was more than I could handle.

He continued to spew out a stream of unintelligible obscenities as he rose to his feet. He slammed a vicious punch into the wall, leaving a gaping hole. Still yelling and sobbing, he ran around the apartment mourning the death of his mother, with a raw, child-like grief.

Regardless of age, size, or gender, when your mother dies, you are still her child. She was still this big man's mama and her death hurt him to the core.

After about an hour of crying and talking, Bill composed himself and was able to call his uncle. I overheard him say that he would drive home right away, a two-hour drive from Hays, Kansas.

When he got off the phone, I noticed his hand was bleeding. I looked at it and determined he had fractured a bone when attacking the apartment wall. Since Bill did not have a car and further assistance from the girlfriend did not seem forthcoming, I took him to the local emergency room, just as dawn was breaking. While waiting for the cast to be applied, he called a friend, who agreed to drive him home.

As the ER physician finished putting the cast on his broken hand, he asked Bill what he was going to do next. With tears in his eyes, the big football player looked down at the floor and said, "I am going home to bury my mama."

*   *   *

Postscript

Eddie Ford and Bill Walker suffered similar, unexpected personal losses as young men and student athletes. Eddie returned and continued playing; Bill never returned to college or college athletics. They each dealt with grief in their own personal ways and I will always respect that.

11

Cafeteria Chaos
– Food for Thought –

We all do things that we later regret. As a professional teacher and coach, I have certainly made my share of mistakes. Let me tell you about the big mistake I made in the summer of 1984 that almost cost a young man his life. It was as close as I had ever come to actually seeing a person beaten to death. UGLY!

I had been enjoying a delightful summer in the mountains of Colorado, where I was head football coach at Mesa State University. We called this "down time." The last school year had ended; the students had gone home; and the fall season hadn't yet started. All in all, things were looking good. We were coming off a successful season and most of our top players would be returning for another year. A few guys had to attend summer school to get their grades up, but by and large the campus seemed almost deserted and I had very little "babysitting" to do. As one of my colleagues was heard to remark, "Schools are wonderful places when there aren't any students around."

One particular day I was walking from my office to the Student Center. As I entered the building I heard a terrible commotion. Someone was yelling and screaming at the top of his lungs. I could barely make out what the screeching was about, but I knew it meant trouble. I spotted two of my football players, Cedric Logan and Namon Mack, running frantically down the hall. They were the ones making all the noise. Both Cedric and Namon were black players I recruited from Denver. Cedric was a fullback and Namon was a big defensive tackle. Both were very strong. Both needed summer school to be eligible for the next season. Cedric was a good worker and a real team player. Namon, on the other hand, was a little lazy. He weighed about 290 pounds, which was probably 20 to 30 pounds overweight. Both were tough guys who were brought up in the inner-city.

As I approached the two enraged players, I could see blood streaming down Cedric's face. He looked like he had just gone ten rounds with Mike Tyson. He was screaming, "Where is that muddafuckah? I'll kill that bastard!"

Cedric had worked himself into such a rage that I couldn't get him to settle down and tell me what the problem was. I tried to grab him but he just pulled away and continued storming around like a lion on the scent of its prey. He just kept on yelling and screeching, "I'll kill that muddafuckah! I'll kill him!"

That's how I knew he was out of control. Besides the blood on his face, that is. Normally if I would ask him to stop and talk to me he would have done so. But not this time. He was really steamed. Meanwhile, Namon kept moving around also. He acted like a hound dog sniffing for a raccoon. Finally I got a tight hold on Cedric so he couldn't get away. I asked him to settle down. "Let me know what happened so I can help you," I told him.

"That son-of-bitch sucker-punched me," Cedric finally replied.

"Who did?" I asked.

"I don't know his name, but that bastard is going to pay!" he said. "Look at me. I am bleeding like a stuck pig."

Namon, who was still searching for the unnamed assailant, came over when I called him to help me sort this thing out. "Namon, tell me what happened."

"All I know is what Cedric told me," Namon replied. "Some guy he was talking to hit him in the face. I was walking to class when I ran into Cedric and saw him bleeding."

"Who hit him and where is he?" I asked.

"He ran into the student union after he sucker-punched me," Cedric said. "I think he may be hiding in here someplace, and when I find him I am going to mess him up for life."

I knew he would, too, now that he had Namon by his side.

Part of my job was to protect my players, even if that meant protecting them from their own stupidities. I decided to talk to the other guy to get his side of the story. It just didn't make sense to me that some guy Cedric was talking to would suddenly punch him in the face, unprovoked. "You both stay here!" I ordered.

"NO!" Cedric yelled. "I want that muddafuckah."

"Cedric," I yelled in my most authoritative voice, "You and Namon stay here! I'm going to look for the guy in the cafeteria."

The cafeteria was very dark when I entered. The only light was coming from a large window. I strained to see if anyone was there. While scanning the poorly-lit room I heard a noise coming from my far right. As I approached I could make out the silhouette of a person standing in the corner. Coming closer, I could see that this person was black and wore a pair of leather half-gloves with the fingers cut out—the kind that weight lifters often wear. He stood about 6'1", was well-muscled, and looked to be very familiar around a weight room.

"Who are you?" I asked.

No response. I then said, "Tell me what happened."

Still no response. "I know you didn't just hit Cedric for no reason, tell me what happened," I demanded again.

Finally the guy said, "It is none of your business!"

It was obvious that he was irritated. He was alternately clench-ing and unclenching his fists, causing me to think of what Cedric had told me - namely, that he was just talking with this guy when the guy hauled off and sucker-punched him. I wondered if he was about to do the same to me.

My gut told me that I'd better get one off before he got one on me. I quickly threw a punch that caught him squarely on the chin. Down he went. Next, I moved in to get on top of him, but this guy was no stranger to street fighting. He rolled away and then stood up, while my 45-year-old body stumbled to the floor. I remember thinking that in my younger days I would have been all over this guy. He started to kick me. I knew I was in trouble so I curled up in a fetal position, to protect my head. However, with my arms and hands covering my ribs and head, I had no way of lifting myself up. He continued to kick away. Fortunately, my assailant was wear-ing tennis shoes and wasn't able to land solid kicks on me. None of them did any real damage.

The kicks stopped after a few seconds, followed by a loud com-motion. I carefully peeked out between my fingers to see what was happening. Cedric and Namon had come to my rescue and were yelling obscenities at the person who was now attacking their coach. They interpreted the situation as one that gave them the green light to assist, without suffering negative consequences.

When I finally got to my feet, I could see the stranger lying on the floor with blood covering his face. Cedric was kicking him and because the guy was seemingly unconscious, he could not protect his face as I had personally done just minutes before. Cedric's kicks were doing significant damage and strange, wheezing sounds were coming from the man on the floor.

Meanwhile, Namon had grabbed one of the metal chairs and was holding it up over his head, waiting for Cedric to back off so he could crush the defenseless body. I was scared since I knew I couldn't stop both Cedric and Namon from doing more damage. With few options, I threw myself on the motionless body and tried to cover him up with my frame. I knew it would be difficult for my two players to get to this guy while I was draped around him. I shouted for them to stop. The gurgling sound coming from the man's throat continued. I was sure he was dying.

Everything came to a sudden standstill when three custodians entered the scene. Hearing all the commotion coming from the cafeteria, they rushed in, turned on the lights and calmed down my two out-of-control athletes.

"Call the police and get an ambulance here as quickly as possible," I said.

The ambulance arrived within a short period of time. By this time the stranger had regained consciousness but was still immobile. The police arrived shortly thereafter and questioned me. I told them that the stranger threw the first punch. The police asked if I wanted to press charges and I said that I did. Cedric was also asked if he wanted to press charges, and he too agreed. Before carting the guy off to the emergency room, the officer in charge told me the guy was not even a student and had no business on campus.

Shortly thereafter, I got a phone call from Dr. John Tomlinson, president of the college. He wanted to see me in his office as soon as possible. I thought that this summons could mean trouble. Tomlinson was a good man and a good college president. He was anxious to hear what had taken place earlier in the day. "Bob, tell me what happened this afternoon in the cafeteria," he asked.

I gave him a full and mostly-accurate accounting of the event - except that I omitted the part about who threw the first punch.

Tomlinson looked me square in the eye and asked me to tell the story again. "Don't leave anything out and don't lie about anything. Did you hit him or did he hit you first?"

I knew he wanted the truth, and even though I was embarrassed about my firing the first punch, I had to be truthful about what actually happened. I told him I did punch the guy first but I was actually convinced he was ready to strike, based on what Cedric had told me and the fact that he kept clenching his fist.

Tomlinson smiled a great smile of relief. It turns out that they had an eyewitness–a woman who worked in the cafeteria. She had been cleaning tables in a darkened area when the situation developed. Since she did not know what had transpired earlier, it seemed as though I was the instigator and started the whole mess. By my telling the truth, even though it was embarrassing at the time, Tomlinson made it clear that I had saved my job. He would not have been able to keep a head football coach who was a proven liar, no matter how many games he won. President Tomlinson advised me to drop the charges I had filed with the police and let the matter die a natural death.

I called Cedric and convinced him also to drop the charges against the guy. Cedric agreed and we called the police department to do so. The officer in charge told me the stranger was doing better and they now had him in a cell. He also told me the guy was from Colorado Springs and had a record of assault in two other cases. After we dropped the charges, the police let him go with a warning and like the sheriff in the old west, told him to get out of town.

I never saw or heard anything about the situation again.

* * *

Postscript

I never learned what actually took place that summer afternoon between Cedric and his assailant. I do know that whatever caused the problem did not warrant a loss of life.

12

Rules Are Rules

While working under Head Coach Bill Mallory at the University of Colorado, I learned many things that influenced my own coaching philosophy. One of his disciplinary practices, known as "Dawn Patrol" made such an impact on me that I continued his legendary strategy later in my own coaching career. The following two stories demonstrate the effectiveness and sometimes humorous side-effects of "Dawn Patrol."

Dawn Patrol
– The Most Dreaded Punishment –

After a dozen years in the high school coaching ranks, I finally worked my way up to my first college gig. In 1978, Bill Mallory hired me to be running back coach at my alma mater, the University of Colorado.

Coach Mallory was very intense. A very good man, but you sure as hell didn't want to get on his bad side or he would run your ass into the ground, literally.

Colorado had just signed a great talent, Gary Turner, who was a *Parade All-American* out of St. Louis. And since he was a running back, he became my responsibility.

Coach Mallory had his eye on Gary as soon as he reported to camp. Gary was 20 pounds overweight, and at 5'11", weighed about 200 pounds, though his ideal playing weight was about 180. So my job was to get Gary back in shape, just as it was to punish any of the running backs when they broke the rules.

The coach had a pre-game routine when we played at home. On the morning of the game the staff would meet at our favorite greasy diner. Our third game that season was against the University of Miami. The morning before the game, Coach Mallory made a point to sit by me, and I could tell something was eating at him. "Bob," he said, before I even had time to drink my orange juice. "You know your Turner missed curfew last night."

I nodded in disbelief. Coach Mallory always made it sound like our position players were our very own children.

"You get that little S.O.B. up for Dawn Patrol tomorrow," he said. "I'll run his little ass until his tongue hits the ground. And I don't care whether we win or lose this afternoon, you both better be there."

Dawn Patrol. Those two words could bring a player to his knees. And it wasn't any easier on the position coaches.

Coach Mallory had two ways of disciplining players. The first was if the player broke a minor rule, he would be required to run what was called "Buff Reminders" which were a series of sprints following a full practice. The second, more severe form of punishment was the Dawn Patrol, which required a 5 a.m. run with Coach Mallory, who normally ran two to three miles every morning. It was the duty of the position coach to make sure the player was at the track on time, which meant waking up at 4 a.m. Mallory operated on the theory that if the position coach had to get up that early, he would try extra hard to get that player to follow the rules, so it would not interfere with his own sleep in the future.

As the players entered the locker room for pre-game meetings, I pulled Gary aside. "Coach Mallory wants you at Dawn Patrol at 5 a.m. tomorrow," I yelled. "You better be there on time or I will put your ass on a bus and send you back to St. Louis. You got that?"

Gary sheepishly nodded as if he understood the severity of his actions. Coach Mallory, Gary, and I were all at the stadium at 4:45 a.m. the next day. Being a Sunday morning, my family and I planned to go to church at 7 a.m., after which, I would go home, change my clothes, and be back in the office by 9 a.m. to work on the next opponent. So, I figured it would be a smart idea to just wear my church clothes to Dawn Patrol.

Everything started fine. Coach Mallory and Gary were going to run eight laps — two miles — and then I would be off to pick up the family and head to church. I was surprised that Coach was only going to run two miles. The victory over Miami (17–7) made me think, *Coach must be happy we played so well yesterday. He's taking it easy on Gary.*

After the first lap Coach Mallory was about 70 yards ahead of Gary. I was leaning against a wall that surrounded the field and was actually thinking about the previous day's win and what we needed to do to beat our next opponent. Then Coach Mallory ran by me for the first time and said, "Bob, get Gary to run faster and try to keep up with me."

I knew that was going to be hard for two reasons. First, Gary was one of those guys who could run very fast, but only for a short distance. He was not a long distance guy like Coach Mallory. Gary probably had never run a full mile in his life, much less two. Second, Coach Mallory was a strong runner - he ran about fifteen miles a week - so two miles were easy for him. It would be a hard pace for

Gary to keep.

"Pull the lead out," I yelled as Gary passed. "Pick up the pace and get up there with Coach Mallory."

Gary turned and looked at me like I was crazy. "I can't keep up with him," he replied.

"You damn well better!" I screamed.

As Coach Mallory finished his third lap, Gary had fallen behind by more than 100 yards. "Bob," he growled. "Get him to at least make an effort to try to keep up. He's just trotting." I could tell he was getting pissed because of Gary's lack of effort.

As Gary slowly passed me, I told him to pick it up. He looked at me as if I was asking him to do the impossible. "Pick it up!" I shouted.

Coach Mallory was getting stronger as the run continued. I was starting to get nervous because Gary was really starting to struggle.

On his sixth lap, Coach Mallory was fuming. "If I lap this sonofabitch before we finish, I am going to send his ass home and fire you. That's not a joke, that's a freakin' promise," he roared. "Now get off your ass and get him to run."

As I sprinted onto the track I realized that Gary was now 300 yards behind and he looked as if he was carrying a piano on his back. I figured Coach Mallory would just about lap Gary at the end of his final lap.

I decided to change my approach. Instead of criticizing Gary, I would encourage him. "Come on Gary, you can do it. You don't have much left," I shouted. It seemed futile though since Gary was slowing down and starting to walk. I could see my first college coaching job disappearing out the window. I began to jog alongside Gary, doing everything in my power to get him through the race without being lapped.

"It's no use, Coach," he cried. "He's gonna catch me. I can't run this far. Maybe I'm not cut out to be a Buffalo. Just let me stop and send me home."

"That's nonsense, Gary. I know you can, just keep running," I said.

"No, Coach," he said. "Let me go, I don't belong here." Now I was running and holding onto his arm trying my best to pull him the final 400 meters.

All the while Coach Mallory was screaming at us in the background. "I'm going to catch you; I'm going to catch you!" he shouted.

I couldn't see how far we were ahead of Coach Mallory, but he was close enough that I could hear him breathing heavily.

Finally, as we made the turn leading into our final lap, I saw that Coach Mallory was 100 yards back. "We're going to beat him, Gary. Just keep running," I said.

Somehow Gary found his second wind and pulled away from me and crossed the finish line before Coach Mallory could lap him. He still had one more lap to go, but he didn't let Coach catch him.

I was in terrible shape, and running that quarter of a mile with Gary had taken its toll on me. I was sweating profusely and breathing like I had just finished a marathon. I dropped to the ground to try and catch my breath.

Coach Mallory looked at me huffing and puffing on the ground. He started towards the locker room, then paused, turned, and remarked: "You better get in better shape if you're going to continue coaching in college."

Postscript

My wife saw me when I came home to change clothes for church. I was a mess; my hair was disheveled; my clothes were drenched with sweat; and I looked like I had just gone 10 rounds in the ring with André the Giant. She shook her head and then asked if I was still excited about being a college football coach.

* * *

The Drowning

– Terror in the Deep –

It was late November, just after the Thanksgiving holiday. Temperature was in the low teens. A faint residue from a two-day-old blizzard still blanketed the frozen turf. Grand Junction, Colorado, was experiencing an atypical cold spell for this time of year.

I was not happy. Alone and freezing, I found myself out at the practice field at 5:15 a.m. on this dark and dreary morning. But rules are rules. Lonnie Williams, my star running back, had broken a team rule and was due to meet me here to run his Dawn Patrol. Since I had witnessed first-hand how well it worked for Coach Mallory when I was his assistant coach, I was convinced it could work in my football program too.

"Where the hell is he?" I muttered to myself, checking my watch one more time, knowing that I would be really ticked off if he didn't show.

In my two years of coaching, I had learned that three elements were critical for developing a winning college football team: discipline, control and structure. We had just ended our regular season with a victory and I had given the players Thanksgiving week off. The week following Thanksgiving we would play our first play off game. I told the players that they could go home for the holiday but that they needed to be back in school and ready for practice by the following Monday. No exceptions!

Unfortunately, Lonnie could not get back from California in time for that Monday practice. His flight schedule routed him through Salt Lake City, where heavy snowfall forced a postponement of his connecting flight into Grand Junction. It was a tough call to make, but when rules are broken consequences must be paid. One of the consequences for breaking a rule on my team was Dawn Patrol.

Dawn Patrol was not a complicated punishment. The player would meet me at the practice field at 5:30 a.m. and I would supervise his two mile run. Obviously, the two mile jaunt for a conditioned athlete wasn't that big a deal. But getting up and out there before dawn was another matter. Everyone hated that early morning date with the coach.

A car drove up. It was Williams. The snow crunched beneath my footsteps as I approached his vehicle. It wasn't windy but the temperature was bitter, bitter cold. My breath circled above like puffs of steam.

"Hey, Lonnie, glad you're on time. Let's get it over with. You know the drill," I barked.

"Coach, I am so sorry, man, but it wasn't my fault that my plane was delayed," he pleaded. "You know I never miss practice. Do I have to do this?"

Lonnie's voice sounded like gravel and he coughed and sniffled. I collected my thoughts. "You feeling okay?" I asked.

"Yah, I'm just coming down with the crud, I guess. My whole family had it. I'll be okay."

My mind suddenly shifted into fast forward. Not a good thing having your star running back feeling under par just when the national playoffs were about to begin. On the other hand, it would set a bad precedent if I were to let Lonnie off the hook for his rule infraction. That would be like cutting off my nose to spite my face. So I quickly came up with Plan B.

"You know - I have a better idea. Let's head over to the field house and we'll just let you swim laps for 20 minutes or so. Water exercise may do your body a little good, considering all the pounding it normally takes. Besides, I don't want you catching pneumonia on me. You understand, son?"

Instead of the grateful response I expected, Lonnie reacted with fear and panic. "Oh no, no, no, no! Please, no! Coach, I don't like the water. Coach, I hate the water! I would rather run, please."

"What's going on here?" I asked. "I try to offer you a compromise and you hit the panic button. Is there something I should know?"

"Coach, you know black people don't like water. We don't like swimming. You aren't being fair on this at all." Lonnie grew angrier as he pled for mercy and begged for any kind of punishment other than swimming.

By now, my patience was wearing thin. I was not pleased to be up so early in the cold, dark morning because of this player's punishment. And I was doubly mad that now he was trying to talk me out of it by giving me this "blacks can't swim" excuse.

"Strip down and get your ass in the pool, you little baby!" I yelled, as we entered the field house. "You can jog in the pool for 45 minutes instead of swimming for 20 minutes. You don't have to swim, just jog. Got it? You're wearing me thin, Lonnie."

It was dark in the pool area. There were two night lights on, one at each end of the pool. I didn't know where the switches were but it was just illuminated enough that I could keep track of him during his work-out.

"Jump in! Your 45 minutes will start then. Hurry up!" I ordered. To my amazement, Lonnie dove in. I expected him to jump in feet first, considering all his complaining about being a poor swimmer. After he hit the water, I could see him swim the width of the pool and within just a few seconds it seemed he was back up out of the water and screaming. He looked like he just streaked through the water and was immediately back up on the other side. I wanted to chuckle but he was so upset and terrified of something.

I yelled, "Get your butt back in the pool and start jogging!" I wanted Lonnie to know that I was getting pretty exasperated with this Dawn Patrol thing.

He kept yelling something I couldn't really understand. He was screaming and obviously afraid of something he was pointing to in the water.

"Slow down. What is it?" I yelled.

"Something is swimming in the water. It's a shark or an octopus or something. Something is in there swimming and I am not going back in there! I know it is alive, Coach. Holy crap!" Lonnie screamed.

I naturally assumed he was just jerking me around, trying to pull something on me. Because the pool area was so dimly lit, I couldn't see the far end of the pool from where I was standing. I made my way grudgingly to the other end. Sure enough. Something was there. But what? I could see a dark shadow moving around slowly back and forth. I squinted in an attempt to focus. It looked like a body.

"Oh, my God, it looks like a body!" I screamed. "Lonnie, find the lights, hurry."

As I got closer, I could see the outline of a head, two arms and two legs. The adrenaline rushed through my body as I tried to think what to do. I saw Williams sprinting for the exit. He wasn't about to stick around with the potential of a corpse in the pool.

"Lonnie, call the campus police!" I screamed after him as he raced down the hall.

Then I realized he wouldn't have a key so I ran out of the pool area and down the hall to my office. I figured if the poor soul had been under water this long he or she was surely dead and anything else I might be able to do would be of little help.

Just stay calm and get the police here as quickly as possible, I thought. I dialed the campus police and, to my surprise, had an answer on the second ring.

"This is Coach Cortese," I said, trying to sound calm. "I am over here in Saunder's Field House and was just in the pool area and saw a body floating around in the bottom of the pool."

"Please repeat that, Coach," said the male voice on the line.

"It's a body, a body, is floating around on the bottom of the pool over here in Saunder's Field House," I screamed. "This is no bullshit, get someone over here immediately and call for an ambulance. I am not screwing around. Hear me?"

"Okay, Coach. Hang on the phone and we will get someone over there as quickly as we can."

It took about three or four minutes to get a response. The campus police arrived first followed by the Grand Junction City Police. It wasn't long before four or five uniformed police officers were storming down the hall toward the pool area.

Not being that much into death and dead bodies, I lingered in my office for a few minutes but then headed down to the pool area as I knew the officers would want me to give a statement about the discovery. I could see all the lights were now on and as I approached the pool's entrance, two policemen came out the door, roaring with laughter. One was dripping wet from head to toe and obviously had been the one who retrieved the body.

I was so confused. At a time like this, laughter did not seem appropriate. The two officers could hardly stop enjoying the moment and it took a few seconds for them to contain themselves.

"What happened? What did you find?" I questioned after the hilarity subsided.

"Coach," said the drenched cop, "it was the mannequin from the Red Cross class - you know - what they use to practice CPR. Well, it was all tangled up in the pool sweep. You weren't seeing things. It was the pool sweep moving the 'body' around as it cleaned the pool bottom." And then he started roaring again.

Postscript

Two days later, when I was heading home for the day, I found the mannequin in the passenger seat of my car. Some jokester had pinned a note on it that read, "Thanks for saving my life!"

The day following this incident, I met Lonnie outside at the practice field and watched him run his two miles. He was really bundled up.

13

Mixed Messages

– The Power of Words –

Early in my coaching career, I learned that a football coach has to be careful what he says around young athletes. Well-intended words can sometimes result in unintended, unpredictable, and unfavorable consequences as well.

Case in point: I was head coach at Mesa State College in Grand Junction, Colorado, throughout the decade of the 1980s. Johnny Pagano was a freshman backup middle linebacker. He was a good—but not great—player. He stood about 5'11" and weighed 205. Johnny wasn't very big, and not very fast, but he had a knack for being in the right place at the right time.

Johnny's parents, Sam and Diane Pagano, were among my dearest and best friends. I was there when Johnny was born and watched him grow up. I felt like part of the family. Since the time he could walk, Johnny had been around football. His dad coached high school football in Colorado and Johnny always tagged along. He tagged along to practices and games, and ended up playing for his dad in high school. And as I mentioned, Johnny was a good player, but not great. When I recruited Johnny Pagano, a lot of people thought I signed him because of my relationship with his father. Not true. I signed him because I believed he could help our team. More about Johnny later.

As a head football coach, you have to be careful what you say around young men. For an athlete to still be playing the sport when he reaches the college level, it means he has dedicated a huge part of his young life to being successful in the sport. And more often than not, these young athletes have gone above and beyond what is required.

As a coach, you must recognize that when you over-emphasize something, many athletes will strive to meet your expectations. However, there can be a downside to this. What happens when it is not possible for a particular athlete to achieve the stated goals? Or what if there is an easier way to attain these goals and the athlete chooses the route that goes against everything you've taught him, just so he can please you?

While I was the head football coach at Mesa State College, we won many games. Naturally, I was fortunate in having some very good players, as well as excellent assistant coaches. In the 70s and 80s everyone knew how important it was to get bigger, stronger, and faster. Universities like Brigham Young and Nebraska set the standard. My staff and I spent time at both schools trying to learn better ways to help our players reach their full potential. A group of strength coaches from BYU even developed a training program called *BIGGER, STRONGER and FASTER*. Every month these coaches published a magazine that offered coaching tips on certain lifts and drills designed to help athletes become better football players. Since I was a copycat, I followed their tips and routinely quoted their motivational words to our players.

It was also during this era that steroids were just starting to concern most college coaches, however, not at today's level. We knew that it was illegal to use them without a doctor's prescription, which should have been a deterrent in itself. We also believed the horror stories about how unhealthy it was to use them.

While a member of Coach Bill Mallory's staff at the University of Colorado, I learned the importance of working with players during the off-season. Coach Mallory taught me to run an off-season program that would improve the players in significant ways. During the off-season we wanted our players lifting, running, doing plyometrics, and working on agility. Our players knew that if they wanted to play, they needed to buy into our off-season program and most of them did.

We worked our players very hard during the off-season. We wanted everyone to get better. Our philosophy was that each player had to improve in three areas. Players had to increase their lifts, gain muscle, and become lighter on their feet. Weightlifting was eminent in our program, since we always stressed the importance of getting bigger and stronger.

Many of our players were strong in the weight room. And because steroids had become so prevalent in weight rooms across the country, we took every precaution to make sure they didn't wind up in ours. We ardently believed that taking steroids was not an option for our athletes, so we talked to them constantly about our zero tolerance policy for shortcuts through the use of illegal substances. We brought in doctors, weightlifters, and exercise specialists to discuss the health risks resulting from steroid usage. In addition, we threatened our athletes with steroid testing and ultimate suspension from the team, should a test prove positive. At the time, however, there was really no way we could afford to test our players for any kind of drugs, no less steroids. Our budget simply did not include funding for such expensive tests.

My approach was to counsel and threaten in hopes that the players got the message. However, we still preached getting bigger, stronger and faster. "But don't take steroids," we warned.

One day I was in the weight room putting the players through their workouts when I noticed that our freshman backup middle linebacker was goofing around and not really lifting with any effort. It was Johnny Pagano, the son of my old friends from Colorado. I recruited Johnny because I thought he could help our team. Most people assumed that since he didn't have the "measurables" that many coaches look for in a high school linebacker, that I signed him because of my relationship with his father. As mentioned earlier, this was simply not the case. I really believed he could help us. Although he wasn't very big or very strong, his high school record really did demonstrate that he had a knack for being in the right place at the right time.

I loved Johnny very much and thought of him as a relative in addition to being a player on my team. Sometimes I had to come down on him pretty hard for not being committed enough during the off-season, but I knew he could handle it and most of the time he did. When Johnny got to Mesa State, lifting weights was not his forte. He wasn't very strong and was embarrassed that players not of his caliber were stronger in the weight room.

One particular day during our off-season weight room workouts, I grabbed him and pointed out that next year he was going to have to compete for the starting middle linebacker position. He would be up against a junior named Blake, who was 6' 4" and weighed 235 pounds. Blake was very fast and was a horse in the weight room. He was well-built and held some of our weightlifting records. He was a weightlifting fool. When he got in the weight room, he was there to work – no B.S. Johnny, by contrast, came into the weight room only because we required him to be there. He put such little effort or intensity into his lifting that he hardly broke a sweat. I was upset with Johnny that day because he was his usual self — not working as hard as I thought he needed to. I told him he better get with it or he might never play at Mesa State.

"Look at that guy lift," I barked at him as I pointed at Blake, who was working hard. "He wants to be good and is paying the price now so that he can play well next season. If you worked like he did in the off-season you could make yourself stronger, which would enable you to be a better player," I said. "You will never get any bigger, stronger or faster with the lackluster effort and attitude you have about lifting weights."

When the workout was over, I went to my office and was soon startled to see Johnny at my door. "Coach, you got a second?" he stammered.

"Sure, come on in," I answered. "What's up?"

"Coach," he began, "I am going to start taking steroids."

"Are you crazy?" I shouted. "There is no way I would ever allow you to do that. What about your mother and father, how do you think they would react?"

"You know how you keep preaching for us to get bigger, stronger, and faster?" he asked. "Well, I am never going to be as tall as Blake, but you keep comparing me to him. The only way I am going to get close to his strength and weight is to do what he is doing. So in order for me to compete with him I need to take steroids - like he does."

Stunned, I asked, "What are you talking about?"

"Blake is who you compare me to and who I have to compete with in order to start next year. I guess that means I need to do what he is doing in order to be 'the man,'" he said. "You know that football is very important to me. I want to be a great player and so I need to get bigger and stronger. I realize that. Steroids will enable me to be what I want to be and what you expect me to be."

We talked for over an hour about steroids and hard work. By the time we were finished Johnny had decided against taking steroids and committed to working hard - to be as good as he could naturally be.

Johnny did improve his attitude and increase his efforts in the weight room. He really never got much bigger but did improve his strength over the course of four years at Mesa State. As a senior, Johnny was a Second-Team All-American and an All-Conference linebacker.

Challenging players to get bigger, stronger, and faster and at the same time admonishing the use of steroids, is not a good strategy. Players know that steroids enable them to achieve what most coaches want them to accomplish during the off-season. They know steroids are a shortcut to becoming bigger and stronger players.

As coaches, we have to be careful what we ask our players to do.

* * *

Postscript

Johnny Pagano turned out to be one of the best linebackers I ever coached. On the field he was so smart that he could offset some of the physical tools that he lacked. He was a coach on the field. He knew what every single player should do. He studied films relentlessly and was able to figure out what the opponents were trying to do.

Oh yes, I forgot to mention he was a tough nut. He is now a successful coach in the NFL, as an assistant with the San Diego Chargers.

14

Forecasting Skills

– Interpreting Mother Nature –

After 12 years coaching high school football, I was ready for the "big-time" or so I thought. Bill Mallory, head coach at the University of Colorado, hired me as an assistant coach at my alma mater. My assignment was to coach running backs and help with recruiting in the states of Colorado, Wyoming and Utah.

Coach Mallory was a very intense and highly-organized individual. He expected the same from his players and coaches. Shortly after he hired me, he gave me a list of all the things he expected me to do as an assistant on his staff. Then we met to discuss the duties. The list went something like this:

1. Coach running backs

2. Recruit Colorado, Wyoming, Utah

3. Handle all summer jobs for players

4. Organize and run summer football camp

5. Help supervise off-season weight program

6. Attend all booster club meetings

7. Weather

I was quite comfortable about my ability to perform six out of seven of these jobs. I didn't fully understand what Coach Mallory meant by the last item on the list - weather. He explained that Colorado weather was highly unpredictable throughout the day, particularly in the spring and fall months. Since the University was located in Boulder, someone was needed to call the local weather bureau each morning that practice was scheduled to get an up-to-the-minute forecast. That someone was me.

This weather information was used by the staff to plan the afternoon's practice session. For example, if the forecast predicted cold temperatures or snow, we could use the field house to practice. If it was too wet, we could use the turf field in the stadium rather than practice on natural grass fields. In addition, the weather forecast provided the information needed to advise the players on what to wear for practice so that they would be prepared for severe weather conditions and dress accordingly.

No problem, I thought. All I had to do was call the weather bureau each morning before the 7 a.m. practice day staff meeting and get the forecast for that afternoon's weather. Unfortunately, it was not as easy as I thought.

I was so excited to be coaching at the college level that I got to the office at 6 a.m. on the morning of my first staff meeting - a full hour early, probably even before some of the other coaches had even tumbled out of bed. I efficiently assembled my materials in the staff room, had four pencils sharpened, obtained two blank notebooks, stuffed a couple erasers in my pocket, picked up my playbook, and strolled into the large meeting room.

It was 6:20 a.m. I was excited about attending my first meeting as a college coach. I chose a seat at the right end of the large executive table that dominated the room. I wanted to have a clear view of every participant as well as the large chalkboard and depth chart.

I was excited, anxious, and a little nervous. I had always dreamt of being a big-time college coach and now I had my chance. To top it off, it was my own alma mater.

Six-forty-five a.m. I was becoming concerned that no one had yet showed up for the meeting. I was sure that football coaches were never late.

Six–fifty a.m. and still no sign of anyone. No Coach Mallory, no assistant coaches, not even a lowly graduate assistant.

Finally, at 6:55 a.m. everyone started bopping in all at once. As coaches showed up, they each went to their respective offices, grabbed a cup of coffee, and entered the meeting room where I had been sitting the past 45 minutes all ready to go.

First off, I was told by George Belu, offensive coordinator and a very good friend, that I wouldn't get to keep the seat I had so carefully chosen. That was Coach Bob Ruebin's seat. Apparently I failed to realize there was a pecking order among coaches for seating positions. Since I was low man on the totem pole, I had to find a place somewhere off to the side that no one else wanted and which afforded no chance of seeing what was going on unless I moved my chair around with each change of agenda item. As a new member of the staff, there was no way I was going to disrupt the established order.

At precisely 6:58 a.m., Coach Mallory entered the room. He dropped a huge stack of paperwork at the head of the staff table where he sat and without looking up, he asked, "Bob, what will the weather be like this afternoon?" Since I was still stewing over the "injustice" of having been dislocated, I wasn't sure I heard him clearly so I responded, "Sorry, Coach, what did you ask?"

"The weather, the weather!" he said impatiently.

The weather? What about the weather? Then it hit me. *Oh, my God!* In my quest to impress my coaching colleagues, I had forgotten to get the information needed to provide the staff with the weather forecast. "It will just take me a minute to call and find out what it will be like this afternoon," I responded as I headed out the door, wishing I could fall through the floor.

I ran down the hall to my office to call the weather bureau. Luckily, I didn't have to waste time to look up the number; I had it on a scratch pad next to my phone. After getting the update for the afternoon practice I ran back down the hall to the meeting room where I repeated the information for all to hear. So much for being the "eager beaver" at the staff meeting! A lot of good it did me.

The next morning I got to the office about 6:30 and had plenty of time to call the weather bureau and get an updated afternoon forecast. When Coach Mallory entered the meeting at 6:58 a.m., the first thing he did was to ask me what the weather would be that afternoon. I proudly reported what the weatherman told me and we proceeded with planning the practice for the day.

My charge was to call only on days we practiced. Since we were in spring ball and didn't practice every day, I did not get a weather report every day.

After two days off, we had our third practice. I was assigned to give all the drills and progression to the entire staff at the meeting. This would be my first time talking football in front of the entire staff. Naturally, I was very nervous about presenting my football ideas to a cadre of coaches who had been coaching at the college level for a very long time. I pushed everything else aside in order to devote my full attention to preparing my presentation.

As usual, Coach Mallory entered the room at precisely 6:58 a.m. "What kind of weather are we having this afternoon, Bob?"

I almost swallowed my tongue! "Shit, I am sorry, Coach," I stammered. Being so anxious to give a knock-out performance to the staff, I had completely forgotten about the weather forecast. The next practice was scheduled for a Monday following a weekend of no practices. I promised myself that I would never again miss calling the weather bureau to get the forecast.

That Monday my son, Jim, had a project due at school - an elaborate miniature cardboard city that he had worked on for three weeks. It was about 4' by 4' and had numerous little cut-outs glued to different parts. My wife did not want him carrying this work of art on the school bus where it might get damaged. She wanted me to drive him to school that day.

I reminded her that I needed to be at the office by 7 a.m. for our daily meeting and I wasn't sure I could do both. She assured me that I could drop Jim off at school and still make it to the office before the meeting started. She thought the school doors opened at 6:30 a.m. so I could drop him off and make it to the meeting on time, since the campus was only 15 minutes away. I agreed.

Jim and I left the house at about 6:10 a.m., which I thought would give me plenty of time. When we got to school, however, we discovered that the doors did not open until 7 a.m.

I freaked out. How was I going to get Jim into school with his project and still make it to the University in time for my meeting? I left Jim in the car, guarding his valuable city of cardboard, while I knocked on every door possible at his school. I knew someone was inside because there were cars in the faculty parking lot. After about 10 minutes, a custodian finally came to one of the doors and opened it to see what I wanted. I told him my problem and he made the executive decision to break the rule and allow a student in the building before the staff arrived.

Despite this unanticipated delay, I still thought I could make my meeting by 7 a.m. I did not want to be late. If there was one thing I already knew about Coach Mallory, it was that he was always very punctual and expected the same from his players and staff.

The 6:30 a.m. traffic in Boulder can sometimes be brutal. It took me a little longer than I had anticipated to reach the parking lot. As I parked my car I noticed that all the other coaches had already arrived and were probably getting their coffee. I sprinted up the stairs to the meeting room, noting that the clock on the wall read 6:57 a.m. Phew – I made it without getting Coach Mallory upset by my lateness.

As I reached my chair at 6:58 a.m., Coach Mallory entered the meeting room, dropped some paperwork on the table and asked, "Bob, what's the weather for today?"

I almost died! Between running across the parking lot and up two flights of stairs, and now being negligent for the third time in reporting the weather, my heart almost stopped. "I'll run down and get it, Coach," I promised. I knew I had screwed up and didn't want to make excuses for being negligent again.

Coach Mallory was obviously upset. He chewed me out in front of the other coaches. "You know Bob, you have been here for four practices and you have missed giving us our report three times already. When you have a job, get it done," he continued. "Coach Milan had the same responsibility for four years and never once, not once, did he miss calling and getting the report for the day." (Milan Voolitich was the coach who preceded me who had just left for the same position at the University of Michigan.)

Contritely, I left the room to call the weather bureau and get the daily forecast.

That afternoon, purely by coincidence, I happened to overhear Coach Belu on the phone with Milan Voolitich. I asked Coach Belu to let me talk to Milan before he hung up. I kiddingly told Milan that his reliable weather reporting was putting a lot of pressure on me. I asked him, "What was it you did each morning to remind you to check the weather forecast each day?"

There was a short pause on the other end of the phone and then I heard his big laugh. "What are you talking about?" he chuckled, "I never once called the weather bureau!"

"Then how did you get your forecast?" I asked.

"I just looked out the window and told Coach Mallory what I thought it was going to be. If I was wrong, which wasn't very often, what could Coach Mallory do? You just blame it on the weather man...or Mother Nature changing her mind."

* * *

Postscript

Coach Mallory was never convinced that Milan didn't actually call the weather bureau each day for the official forecast. After my conversation with Milan, I never again missed providing the weather forecast – even on days when I didn't call the weather bureau.

15

Sideline Coaching

– Don't Mess with the Dentist –

"You're a typical damned parent! You don't know the first thing about the game of football, yet you come out here to tell your son how to play?" Those were the words directed at me by a dentist who also happened to be my son's youth football coach. That same year, 1969, my team played for the state championship in football and I was an elected member of the Coaches' Association. This guy didn't have a clue about my coaching experience but his comments were partially true.

My eight-year-old son was playing Little League football in Boulder, Colorado. Although I had not yet met him, I knew that the coach was a dentist who had only two years of playing experience in high school and one season of coaching eight and nine year olds. It was rumored that he once made second team All-Intramurals at the University of Iowa, but even that had never been confirmed. After he graduated from dental school, this tooth doctor who spent most of his time working in the saliva of others, apparently decided he wanted to be a part-time football coach. So he volunteered to coach kids in Boulder.

Like most high school coaches, I did not get to watch my own sons

play very often when they were growing up. It seems I was more worried about my own team's success than watching my sons participate
in sports. I justified that by claiming this philosophy would someday
result in my being named head coach at Notre Dame. My misplaced
priorities cost my sons the opportunity to have their dad at games.

My youngest son, Jeff, was a good ball player—not great, but
good. He was tough and aggressive for his age, and I thought someday he might grow big enough to play at the high school level.

One Saturday afternoon I did find time to watch my son play a
football game. I was a few minutes late getting to the field and the first
thing I noticed was the cluster of fans standing on the sidelines. Initially, I assumed a player had been hurt and anxious parents had gathered
to see how he was doing. Only later did I learn that in this league it was
customary for parents and friends to stand and watch the game from
the coach's box, whereas at higher levels, of course, spectators must
remain in the stands. Stands are a wonderful way to keep parents from
hearing what coaches actually say to their kids during games. They also
help coaches by preventing them from hearing what highly vocal and
opinionated parents may be saying.

There I was, standing on the sideline next to what I assumed were
other parents watching their 78 pound sons and envisioning their col-
lege-playing futures. Of course I assumed that my son, Jeff, was surely
the best player on the field and a certain NFL prospect.

As I watched the game unfold, I noticed that every time the
quarterback from the other team dropped back to pass (which was
as often as it rains in a desert), Jeff would veer away from the John
Elway wanna-be. He never made an attempt to hurry or sack the
quarterback. As defensive end, he didn't seem to grasp how important it was for him to do so.

I yelled at him to attack the QB and not veer away from him as
he dropped back. "Go after him when he drops back to pass!" I had

to yell loud enough so he could hear me over the mother standing right beside me who was screaming at her son to pull his pants up. Each time I yelled encouragement for Jeff to get after the QB he would look at me, appearing very unsure and somewhat confused. I was shocked. After nine years thinking this young warrior was aggressive, it now seemed to me that he was playing very passively and avoiding the hit on the opposing passer.

A cold feeling came over me as I realized that quite possibly I had misread the toughness of my own son. I had always been sure that he was going to be a good football player because he was not afraid of contact, but now he seemed to be shying away from it. I always believed if a dog didn't fight as a puppy, he probably wouldn't fight as he grew older.

Standing next to me was a gentleman wearing a dress shirt and a green tie. He looked at me a couple of times and finally after my last plea to my son to rush the QB and not veer to the outside, he said, "You're a typical damn parent! You don't know the first thing about the game of football, yet you come out here to tell your son how to play! I am his coach and he is doing exactly what I want him to do when the QB drops back to pass." The dentist/coach, with his green tie, was rightfully in charge.

I turned away very happy. I wasn't happy that my son was being taught to play dumb football, but I was pleased that he was listening to his coach. I was also relieved that he wasn't really scared of contact after all. I could only imagine what went through Jeff's mind when his dad, a high school coach, told him not to do something his dentist/coach instructed him to do. In this particular situation he learned the coach is always right.

* * *

Postscript

Jeff turned out to be a pretty good high school fullback and earned a scholarship to Wichita State University. They dropped football after he left.

16

Mile High Camp
– Mile High Memories –

Football camps were not as commonplace back in the 1970s as they are today. Indeed, there were only a couple such camps back then that were worthy of the name. Sam Pagano observed one on the east coast and decided to establish his own in Colorado in 1972. Sam was a very successful high school football coach. He coached at Fairview High School in Boulder, Colorado, from 1972 until 1993 and won many football games during that time.

Within a couple of years, the camp had grown to be one of the largest of its kind in the nation. For 18 years, I worked the camp with Sam and his family as we built it into something very special. We began at the Colorado School of Mines, moved to Colorado State, and then on to the University of Northern Colorado, as we outgrew each campus.

The football camp experience left a lasting impression on me. My career benefited from the interaction with impressionable and exuberant youngsters as well as from the coaching staff which consisted of premier athletes and coaches from around the country. The following four stories represent the hundreds of experiences I had and enjoyed during almost two decades of summer camps.

* * *

Stronger Than Dirt
– Dealing with Impressionable Young Athletes –

"All right, guys, let's go wake up these sleepyheads!" I said to three little tykes who had made their way into my room during the night. I was in charge of about 200 young campers aged six to 12 that summer. For many of these kids, it was the first time they'd been away from home. So it was not at all unusual for me to be joined by as many as six of these little guys in my room sometime during the night. It must have given them a sense of security – I was kind of a "father figure" to them. As a staff, we did whatever we could to prevent homesickness and keep these guys from going home early.

When I woke up that morning at 5:45, these young warriors were already awake and ready to go play some football. They had their uniforms on and black paint under their eyes. It's a miracle that I managed to sleep as late as I did since the clatter of small football cleats on the old hardwood floors of Murdock Hall was loud enough to wake even the heaviest of sleepers.

Part of my job was to wake up everyone, which included 500 campers ranging in age from six to 18, plus various coaches from high school, college, and professional ranks, along with numerous pro athletes who were working at the camp. I had to make sure all the campers were on the field by 6:30 for their morning run. We ran the campers before breakfast and worked them hard throughout the day. We wanted to make sure that when the lights went out, they were too tired to engage in much tomfoolery.

Waking everyone up was no easy task. We didn't use phones. The phones were all disconnected for the duration of the camp. Instead, we screamed, banged on doors, and blew whistles – doing anything within our power to make sure everyone was up on time. On this particular morning, it was up to me and these three little guys to get the job done.

The boys walked timidly to their first door, where some of the campers were sleeping. The little guys knocked politely and waited for the occupants to answer. No response.

"That's not how you get these sleepyheads awake," I said. "You have to bang on these doors like big, strong men. Show me how strong you are by banging on the doors with a lot of power. I need strong bangs on these doors. Here, let me show you what I mean. This is how hard you bang and kick on the door," I explained, as I turned towards another door where my two sons and the Pagano brothers were sleeping. I doubled up my fist into a hammer, and struck a blow against the paneled door.

The moment my fist struck the door, two things happened. First, the door fell inward into the room with a loud crash; and secondly, peals of laughter came rolling out from inside the room. It didn't take long for me to realize that I'd been had! These four pranksters knew my morning routine and used my predictability to set a trap for me. They simply removed the door from its hinges and propped it up so that the slightest tap would make it fall.

My three little helpers were both shocked by the sudden turn of events and obviously awed by what they perceived to be my extraordinary physical strength. One of them exclaimed, "My God, he barely touched it!" My reputation had been enhanced considerably.

* * *

Heat, Hydration and Priorities

– Rejecting Gatorade –

While the summer months in Colorado aren't as deadly as they are in other parts of the country, hydration is still very important, especially when it comes to the little guys. During one practice, we were nearing the end of an hour-long session in the sun with the seven-to-ten year olds. I thought the heat was starting to take its toll on some of the young campers.

"Okay men," I yelled. "Take a lap around the practice field and when you get back we will break out the Gatorade for everyone."

I blew my whistle and they were off like a herd of buffalo. Their oversized helmets were bobbing and even from across the field I could hear the plastic of their shoulder pads clapping together as they ran. When I turned to grab a cup of iced-down Gatorade, I noticed that one of my players was not running, but rather, was standing next to me.

It was Murphy - otherwise known as "Murph the Turf" - as he had been nicknamed by the coaches. Since Murphy was overweight and did not run very fast, long distances were especially rough on him.

"Come on Murph, get your lap in so you can get your drink of Gatorade," I said, trying to encourage him. "We'll wait for you to finish running."

Murphy calmly took off his helmet but continued to watch the other players running their laps. Then he casually looked at me, glanced over toward the Gatorade, took another glance toward the running players, then calmly and coolly stated, "That's okay, Coach. Thanks anyway. I'm really not thirsty."

What does a coach say to that?

* * *

Benefits for the Best

– When You Just Can't Say "No" –

The personal and professional relationships I developed while working at this camp had a big impact on my coaching career. Sam knew how to hire the best of the best. Our 50 to 60-member staff featured some of the premier high school, college and professional coaches from around the country, as well as some of the most talented pro athletes and former college players. The young players learned from their heroes including Barry Sanders, Rodney Peete, and even the great Steve Young, just to name a few. And it was also fun for the coaching staff to get to know some of these great players personally as they worked at the camp, especially players like Steve Young.

Steve Young had just finished his career at Brigham Young University and had signed a $40 million deal to quarterback the Los Angeles Express of the USFL. While eating breakfast one day, I asked him, "Steve, what's the biggest difference in your life now that you are wealthy and even more famous then when you were in college?"

He paused, put down his fork and replied, "Coach, it's amazing, now that I have more money than I ever dreamed about, I do more and spend nothing."

"What do you mean?" I asked.

"People cater to me now more than ever before," he replied. "My success has gotten me more freebies and comps. Now that I have money to spend, I spend less."

Throughout the ensuing week, I observed first-hand, just what Steve meant.

During a break that afternoon, a group of coaches decided to play a quick 18 holes of golf. Steve said that he would like to play but he had an interview at a local radio station in Greeley. He said he would take a taxi from the station to the golf course if he finished the interview in time.

Coach Ken Milano, a good friend and high school coach in Colorado, told Steve, "No need to take a taxi, I'll let you use my car and I'll hook a ride with someone else. We'll meet you at the course when you are finished."

Next, Steve remembered he didn't have his clubs with him, so he inquired about renting some at the pro-shop. "No way," said Larry Allen, another high school coach. "I'm not playing today, so you can use my clubs. And, by the way, don't worry about the balls, I have plenty."

When Steve arrived in the clubhouse following his interview, the golf pro asked me, "Is that who I think it is?" I nodded. "No shit," he said. "Is that really Steve Young?" I assured him that it was, explaining that we were working a football camp just down the road.

The club pro then approached Steve. "Well, Mr. Young, it is such a pleasure to meet you in person. My father went to Brigham Young University; I am a huge fan," he said. "Please be my guest and play the course free of charge."

"Thanks, but that's not really necessary," Steve replied.

"I wouldn't have it any other way," insisted the pro. "The golf cart is included."

After golf we went into the clubhouse restaurant. Steve ordered a ham and cheese sandwich. When he asked for his bill, the chef came out from the kitchen and asked Steve for his autograph. The chef then tore up Steve's bill, saying," On me, Mr. Young."

Steve turned towards me with an embarrassed look on his face, shrugged his shoulders and said, "See what I mean? I have plenty of money and no one will let me spend it!"

I should have been a famous quarterback.

* * *

Odds in His Favor

– No Collateral Required –

Since Sam owned the camp, he always let his own team attend free of charge. Every year we would get to see his players grow and excel on the field. One of the best players Sam coached was a kid named Tony Boselli. Tony was a big boy. When he graduated from high school he stood 6'6" and weighed around 285 pounds.

I watched Tony grow from his freshman to his senior year. He got bigger and better each season. He had a wonderful disposition and was a pleasure to coach. My early opinion of Tony was that because he was so very humble, shy, and polite, he might lack enough toughness to be really great on the football field. I was wrong. After his high school graduation, he received a scholarship to play at the University of Southern California.

One of the traditions at the Mile High Camp was gathering in the coaches' lounge and playing poker after we put the campers to bed each night. We'd order pizza, crack open a few adult beverages, and play cards. It was great fun. Many friendships that developed during those late night poker sessions still exist today.

Our group usually consisted of both experienced and very novice players trying their hand at winning a few extra bucks. I was always the banker as well as the mediator of all disputes. They affectionately called me "The Pope" and everyone knew I was in charge.

The coaches' lounge was always off-limits to the players. The staff had to have a place to relax and get away from the campers between practices. We always had a cooler filled with sodas and some other beverages located in the back of the room. The coaches would sit and share different ideas with each other. It was not uncommon, for example, to see the defensive line coach from Penn State working feverishly on the chalk board to show a coach from Texas A&M the drills and techniques he was using.

Following Tony's junior year at USC, Sam hired him to work as a camp counselor at Mile High Football Camp, where he had spent four years as a high school player and camper. Camp counselors were paid $50 a week and did a lot of the "gopher" jobs the coaches found burdensome.

During his days as a mere camper, Tony always wanted to see what was going on in the coaches' lounge. After all, this was where the NFL players who worked the camp would relax after practice. Tony knew that some of his heroes often hung out there and he frequently tried to sneak in to see them. He became a regular pain in the butt. He knew about our big card games and once confided that he could hardly wait until he was old enough to play cards and hang out with the coaches and staff members.

"Can I play cards tonight?" Tony asked me at dinner on his first evening as a counselor.

"Not tonight," I told him. "Too many coaches want to play."

He was obviously disappointed. "Well, how about tomorrow night?"

"We'll see," I replied.

Tony came to me the following night and again asked if he could play cards with the staff members. I replied, "Yes, if you have $50 for buy in." Everyone had to buy $50 worth of chips just to make the game interesting. Tony didn't have $50; all he had was $25. Sam gave him an advance on his salary.

It didn't take long to tell that Tony hadn't been around cards very much. He was like a sheriff. He called every pot trying to keep everyone honest. Eventually he went broke.

Since I was the banker, Tony asked me if he could get another $50 worth of chips. "Sure," I said, "Where's your money?"

He hemmed and hawed a bit, then confessed that he only had the $25 coming at the end of the week. I gave him another $25. He went through that like shit through a goose.

Broke again, he asked, "Can I borrow another $50?"

"When will you pay me back?" I questioned.

"When I get home I will send you $50 right away," he said.

I joked, "It is not good practice to loan someone money, especially when that person doesn't even have a full-time job." Then I said, loud enough for everyone in the room to hear, "Okay Tony, before I risk loaning you money, I need you to answer some credit questions. What does your father do for a living?"

"He owns 15 McDonald's restaurants," he replied.

"Okay, that is strong in case you default on your loan," I said. Next I asked, "What are you going to be doing when you get out of school?"

"I hope I am going to play football in the NFL," he responded, quite forcefully.

"Hmmmm," I muttered. "What round do you think you will be drafted?"

"I hope I am the first or second player drafted," he replied.

"Hmmmm. And how much money does that mean if you are drafted that high?" I asked.

"Somewhere around eight or nine million dollars, I hope." The room filled with laughter.

"Okay," I said. "I'll loan you the $50."

* * *

Postscript

Even though they might not have known it at the time, my young camper/players made just as much of an impression on me as I hope I did on them. They energized me each summer with their commitment and sense of fun. And the camp experience was enhanced by athletes like Steve Young and Tony Boselli. Steve was named National Football League MVP in both 1992 and 1994.

He was also the MVP in Super Bowl XXIX and was inducted into the NFL Hall of Fame in 2005. After graduating from USC, Tony signed the largest contract in NFL history for an offensive lineman – an eight-year, 17 million dollar deal. He was a five-time Pro Bowl selection, and was the first player ever selected by the Jacksonville Jaguars. Today, Tony owns several Whataburger Restaurants in the Jacksonville, Florida area.

17

Dropping Out of Sports for Life
– Misguided Aspirations –

The mass was for Jerry Vito (not his real name per his family's request). After mass ended, my wife asked if I was going to go the cemetery for the burial. It was a very sad day. It's always traumatic when you bury a 16-year-old, but this was extra hard for me because Jerry had been almost part of my family from the time he was seven years old until he was 10.

I told my wife I had to get back to school so I wouldn't be able to join the procession to the cemetery. I expressed condolences to Molly Vito, Jerry's mom. As I held her hand, she whispered something about the importance of loving them while they're still here.

On the drive back to school I remembered the day young Jerry quit Little League baseball. I could remember it as clearly as if it happened yesterday even though the event took place six years earlier.

* * *

"What time do the boys practice today?" I asked my wife. I had a rare afternoon off from my summer job and thought I would watch my two sons practice Little League baseball.

"They start at 4 p.m.," my wife answered. Then it dawned on her that if I was going to be at the field anyway, there was no need for her to drive as well. "Good," she said. "If you're going to practice I won't have to pick up the RAT PACK. Since it is our turn to drive, you can pick them up and take them all to practice."

The RAT PACK was a name given to a group of seven boys, ages nine and 10. They all lived within two blocks of each other in the Martin Park subdivision of Boulder, Colorado. Jerry was a member of the RAT PACK.

We borrowed the name RAT PACK from a group of Hollywood stars who famously hung out together. That group included Frank Sinatra, Dean Martin, Joey Bishop, Sammy Davis Jr., and others. Like the stars, these kids did everything together. They all went to the same school, played sports together, and slept over regularly at each other's homes. Very seldom did you ever see one without the others. If one went out for wrestling, the others did the same. They all joined the same basketball, baseball, and football teams. When one went to the park, the other six were there as well. Each had his hair cut short and they all wore the same type of clothing. They loved playing together, so much so, that many outsiders thought that they were all related in some manner.

When we arrived at the practice field that fateful day, I went to the bleachers where I could get a good view of the boys going through their drills. I was a little surprised to see Jerry Vito practicing at third base. Although Jerry was a member of the RAT PACK, he was the least athletic of the group. I thought he was better suited for the outfield or maybe even second base, but who was I to question a veteran Little League coach? Their coach was a 35-year-old postman named Clark. I don't remember his last name. Clark had done a good job of teaching the boys how to play the game of baseball.

Molly Vito had just arrived to watch the practice so I asked her, "When did Jerry start playing third base?"

"He has always wanted to play third base," she responded. "His grandfather played third base for UCLA and it has been a dream of his to do the same. Coach Clark is letting him try it tonight. I hope he does well."

Coach Clark hit a slow dribbler down to third base and Jerry missed the ball. It went through his legs out to left field. The coach told Jerry to get his body in front of the ball and even if he didn't catch it cleanly, he would at least stop the ball from going into the outfield. He then hit another ball to Jerry and once again Jerry missed it as it rolled to the outfield. Without raising his voice, Coach Clark told Jerry, "Keep your body in front of the ball, Jerry. It won't hurt you."

Jerry tugged at his hat and got set for the coach to hit him another grounder. By now his eyes were as big as silver dollars, but he was ready to give it another go.

Coach Clark hit another grounder to Jerry and once again Jerry missed the ball. Coach trotted out to third base and very calmly showed Jerry how to get down on the ball and keep it in front of him. "Let's try it again," he said to the youngster and jogged back to home plate.

WHACK. He hit the ball to Jerry again. You guessed it, the ball went through Jerry's legs and out to left field. Without a word, the coach hit another ball to the youngster with the same result.

Even though Coach Clark didn't show anger in either his voice or outward demeanor, I noticed that he was hitting the ball harder and harder. Despite his efforts to not get upset with the struggling young athlete, it appeared that he was boiling over inside. This anger spilled out, not in his voice, but in the way he was hitting the ball. I'm sure the coach did not realize that by the time he hit the last grounder to Jerry, he was hitting the ball so hard that not even a grown man could have caught it.

He finally told Jerry to go play right field. As Jerry trotted sheepishly to his new position, the coach turned to Molly Vito and shouted, "What did I tell you? He can't play third base!" It seemed like he was proving a point. I'm pretty sure Jerry heard the comments the coach directed to his mother. And even worse was the fact that Jerry's friends heard them, too.

Three days later when I came home from work, my two sons came running up to me shouting, "Dad, guess who quit the team today?"

"Who?" I asked.

"Jerry!" said my oldest son. "Can you believe it, Dad? Jerry quit today."

Actually, I wasn't surprised. I knew Jerry hadn't been having much fun playing baseball. He was there because that's where his friends were. He was a 10-year-old kid who had a grown man hit grounders to him that were too hot for him to handle. And to top that off, he had to endure the shame of overhearing the coach tell his mother that he didn't quite measure up.

I never saw Jerry again. After he quit the team he naturally drifted away from the RAT PACK. He had nothing else in common with this group of little jocks. He made new friends and developed new interests.

Over the years, Jerry started hanging out with a group of teenagers who were constantly in trouble at school and with the law. During his freshman year, he was caught joy-riding in a stolen car with a bunch of these so-called new friends.

Six years after he quit the team, he was found dead in the basement of the home of one of these new friends. He died from a drug overdose.

In my opinion, the day that Jerry couldn't field the ball at third base was the day he gave up sports and a healthy future with his friends in the RAT PACK. I believe that day led to his tragic and early death.

* * *

Postscript

Youth coaches are given a tremendous responsibility in working with young adults. I believe if Jerry Vito had experienced more fun and encouragement in playing sports he would have stayed with the RAT PACK and might very well be alive today. Question: Is winning a 10-year-olds' Little League game more important than developing a child's self-esteem?

18

A Coaching Dilemma

— *When Is the Gamble Worth the Risk?* –

Every so often we are given an opportunity to change a young person's life. For coaches, this opportunity comes more often than for most. Indeed, these experiences are among the greatest rewards of being a coach. Many times the coach's personal successes off the field are more enjoyable than his professional achievements on it.

In order to protect the identity of a young man and prevent any future consequences, some names and details have been altered; but otherwise, this story is true.

In 1994, I was the head football coach at Fort Hays State University (Hays, Kansas) and I was in a bind. My athletic director permitted me to have three full-time assistants and two graduate assistants (GAs) working with the program each year. One of my GAs had just graduated at the end of the spring semester and the upcoming season was just months away.

For those not familiar with NCAA Division II football, GAs serve a vital role to the program. They have responsibilities and duties that are assigned to coaches at higher division levels. Because of the importance of the position, we advertised widely so it was well known that we had an opening. We needed to hire someone quickly so he would have the opportunity to learn the system.

In mid-June I got a phone call from a former coach whose name was familiar, though I had never met him in person. He told me that his son, Jack, wanted to become a coach but needed some additional hours to complete his undergraduate degree. He thought it would be the ideal situation if I could hire his son for the GA position.

"No way," I told the coach. "Your son is not qualified. We only hire coaches who are working towards their master's degree, because in order to be paid, they have to teach some physical education classes." I told him to give me a call once Jack had completed his undergraduate degree.

"There has to be something you can do. Look, Jack isn't even going to school now and I'm afraid he won't go back if there's nothing in it for him. You know how it is, school isn't any fun unless you're doing something you love," the coach rambled. "I'm just trying to find something to light a fire under his ass so he can get through school."

I sensed that he was breaking up and I felt for him. I tried to think of some way I might help a fellow coach.

"Maybe we can use him as a student coach," I offered. A student coach does the little things that don't require any actual coaching experience like filming practice and breaking down film. "It's an unpaid position, but I can probably get him a partial tuition waiver for helping us out," I said. I finished by telling him that I needed to get it approved by the athletic director and suggested he call me back in a week or so.

Throughout the week I inquired about Jack and as it turned out two of my assistant coaches knew him. And I also found a player who was on a team with him at a junior college. I questioned them about the basics: character, work habits, loyalty, etc.

"You don't want Jack," one of my assistants bellowed.

"Why not?" I asked.

"Just trust me on this one," he said, as the room filled with laughter.

"Well, let's see, he's an alcoholic with a bit of drug problem," one my players said. "But if that's what you stand for Coach, I understand. He could be better now though, I hear he just got out of rehab for the second time."

I learned more about Jack than I cared to hear. One of my coaches even thought he got busted for selling drugs, plus he had just had a child out of wedlock. By the sound of things, getting through school was the least of Jack's concerns.

True to his word, Jack's dad called me a week later.

I started with a basic approach. I had it all figured out. I told him the athletic director would not grant me permission to have another student coach for the upcoming season.

"I can put Jack through school; that's not going to be a problem if you can just give him something to do," he said, trying to persuade me otherwise.

I stopped him before he could go any further. "I'm sorry, but Jack will not be a member of this program," I said. "I know he's an alcoholic and a drug user. What kind of message would I be sending to kids if I brought him into my program?"

All I could hear was silence on the other end of the line.

After a minute or so the coach composed himself and made one last effort to convince me to change my mind. It was like the All-Pro running back nearing the end of his career, who after years of being the league's top rusher is told by team officials that he's going to have to fight like hell if he wants to keep his job.

"Just give him a chance," he pleaded. "This is it for him. Jack just got out of rehab and he's clean. He's made mistakes; he's not perfect. I'm trying to open some doors for him so he can get on with his life. But if no one gives him a chance, what's the use?"

I could feel my heart drop. Bottom line: I have two sons of my own and in this profession it's damn hard to be both a father and a coach. While you are looking after the lives and futures of 100 kids, it is sometimes easy to overlook your very own. It can happen to any one of us.

I softened my stance and invited Jack and his dad for an interview. I didn't want them to get their hopes up, but since he was the son of a coach, I wanted to give him the courtesy of an interview. I told the coach my conditions. Under no circumstances could he tell Jack that I knew about his past problems. He promised me he would not.

"There's no guarantee," I said. "I really don't think I can bring him into the program at this time."

Interview day arrived. We began with the usual small talk until I eventually got around to asking the questions that I would ask any student applying for the student position.

"How do you plan to do the things necessary to help this football team while finding time to stay on top of your studies?" I asked. "You know, you're going to have to use your time wisely. Good time management is a necessity."

"Well, Jack's always..." were the only words the coach could get out of his mouth before I cut him off.

"Hold on," I interrupted. "I'm anxious to hear how Jack would answer the question, now if you'll please excuse us."

Parents answering questions for their kids has long been one of my pet peeves. It happens all the time on recruiting visits and it bugs the hell out of me. How am I going to gain any insight on how a kid thinks if someone is always answering for him?

Jack's dad quietly left the room.

As we continued, I popped the question, "Have you ever been

involved in excess drinking and drugs?"

He paused for a moment and his eyes began to tear up. "Yes," he replied. He was visually shaken and was obviously not expecting that question. Jack continued by saying that he was clean now and felt sure that he would never take another drink or ever use drugs again.

"How can you guarantee that you won't?" I asked.

"I have to," Jack stated.

"Have you ever been to rehab?" I asked.

"I've been twice. I finished my last stay three weeks ago," he responded.

Then it was time for the big question. "Have you ever sold drugs?" I asked.

It took a while for him to answer but he eventually admitted that he had. His addiction to alcohol tied in with his drug use led to his selling drugs. That was the only way he could make enough money to pay the bills and satisfy his demons.

With that I said, "Jack, I think you have the drive to be a good coach, but your drive to drink excessively, break the law by selling and using drugs is probably too big of a risk for me to take by bringing you into this program." I told him it was way too early to tell if he had really kicked the habit. Two or three weeks did not prove that he had mastered his addiction. "Wait a year or so and then re-apply for a student position," I advised.

Jack clearly grasped the consequences for his past actions, but, like his dad, he felt like his last chance was slipping away right before his eyes. In an attempt to prove his commitment to me, he said that he would pay for us to test him every week. "You choose the doctor or the clinic," he said. "I will find another job to pay for the weekly tests and have the results sent directly to you. If I ever test positive or even sniff a drink or have a beer, you can bounce me from the program. Coach Cortese, I want to learn about coach football from you," he exclaimed.

I looked at him and thought about his father and how much they both wanted a new life for Jack. I called his dad back into my office and told them that I needed a week to think about it and let them know my decision. "I'll call you at the start of next week," I told them as they departed.

It was a big gamble, a huge decision, and I spent a considerable amount of time thinking about it. My conclusion: The Fort Hays State football program did not need Jack, but rather, Jack needed the Fort Hays State football program. My dilemma: Is that good enough reason to take a chance on him?

I talked it over with my athletic director and the president and both thought it would be risky, but they each had faith that I would handle the situation for the benefit of all concerned. Without reaching a decision, I called Jack's dad and told him I would like to meet with both of them again the following weekend, acknowledging that this would require another long drive – two hours each way. I did warn him that I thought hiring Jack would be too big a gamble for me to take. But I assured him that I would continue to think about it and would reach a decision before they arrived. I said that even if I didn't decide to use Jack as a student assistant, driving up and being rejected, though very disappointing, might send a strong message to his son. I wanted Jack to know how much drinking and screwing around with drugs had cost him, and unless he stopped completely, he would continue to cause himself hardships.

The following Saturday both Jack and his father showed up in my office. They impressed me by wearing sport coats and ties. They drove up the night before and got a motel room. It was obvious to me how important this decision was to both of them.

I started the meeting explaining the importance of my role as the head football coach. "I'm obligated to the University and the community to bring in student-athletes and coaches alike, who are of high character," I said. "In order to be a member of this program, you have to walk the line. It doesn't matter how good of a coach or player you are. That doesn't matter to me if you cannot be a good citizen."

After 30 minutes of preaching, I looked at Jack's dad and realized that but for the grace of God, this situation could have happened to me with one of my sons. Here was a man fighting like hell to help his son turn his life around. I could easily identify with the fact that football was a very important part of this dad's life. The dad had now turned to the sport to try to get his son to become a productive citizen once again. Over the course of his career I would have bet that Jack's dad had helped a number of athletes keep their lives on the straight and narrow. In his mind, it was football that could re-direct his son, away from a life that was surely headed for destruction.

Jack's dad wasn't alone in the fight, as it was very evident to me that Jack was also fighting to get back on track. I was not totally convinced he could, but I knew he had the desire. I sat and stared at both of them and asked myself the question: *If it were my son, how would I feel?* Football has been very good to me for many years and in many ways. Here I was with a father and a son — who shared the same passion for football as I do —sitting in front of me begging for my help.

With a lump in my throat, I said, "Jack, I'm gonna stick my neck out for you. Would you like to be a student assistant on my staff?"

"Yes!" he exclaimed, as the two of them jumped up to celebrate.

I raised my hand motioning for them to stop, "Let me finish," I said.

I reached into my drawer and gave Jack a job description for a student assistant, letting him know what his responsibilities would be.

"I'm not messing around with you. There will be no freakin' games. You're on probation and if you ever make a mistake I'll send your ass back home on the first bus out of here," I stated. "I'll never raise my voice at you; I'll just send you home. You already have two strikes against you and the third will be your last."

Jack agreed.

Jack turned out to be a wonderful student coach and a model student. He lived with another student coach, one I trusted and respected. I got daily and weekly reports from the roommate about the life Jack was leading. I also had a weekly meeting with Jack scheduled through the entire year. Each week he would come in and tell me how long he had been sober and clean from drugs.

"It's been 26 weeks since I have been clean," he would report.

To acknowledge a year of sobriety, I invited Jack, his dad, and my other coaches (who by this time knew of Jack's former condition) over to my house for dinner. We celebrated Jack's accomplishment. I had a big cake inscribed with the words "One year and still going strong."

After Jack earned his undergraduate degree, I hired him to be a GA for the next two seasons. He was a great coach and when he finally did leave us, our program missed him dearly.

I remember when he got his master's degree. I took special pride in watching him walk across the stage and receive his diploma. I thought back to the day he and his father sat in my office and asked to be a part of the Fort Hays State football program. It was a win/win situation.

* * *

Postscript

Jack has coached at a number of colleges since leaving Fort Hays State. He is currently a member of a football staff at a well-known university. I would not be surprised to someday see him become a head coach.

19

Team Decision-Making

– Democracy at Its Best –

A great deal of travel is involved when coaching football at the NAIA and NCAA Division 2 levels. For example, neither Mesa State College in Grand Junction, Colorado or Fort Hays State University in Hays, Kansas, had opportunities to fly to our away games. That meant long bus trips were the norm. Many times we had to travel ten to 14 hours just to play an opponent.

Typically, we would board a bus early on Friday mornings and drive all day to get to the location of the next day's game. We would get a motel room that Friday night, get up the next day, play our game, grab a quick bag lunch, and drive straight back to campus.

I always had a strict rule about being on time. If the bus was scheduled to leave at 7 a.m., I expected all players, coaches, and managers to be in their seats and ready to go five minutes before the departure time. No excuses! The bus would leave precisely at the scheduled time.

I never took roll. At the scheduled departure time, I would tell the driver to close the door and start driving. If someone was late – tough! He'd be left behind.

During the 1993 season at Fort Hays State University, we started to pull out of the parking lot on our way to a game with Ft. Lewis College in Durango, Colorado, about a 12-hour drive. I could hear some players whispering about something, so I figured someone didn't make it on time. I only hoped it was a player whose absence wouldn't jeopardize our game. Even though I was concerned, I curled up against the window, closed my eyes, and pretended to sleep.

Tim O'Connor, our defensive coordinator, came up to where I was sitting and whispered in my ear. Our All-Conference starting tailback, Emmett Pride, did not make the bus. Pride was the real deal. He transferred to Fort Hays from Indiana University where he started as a freshman. He was responsible for about 45 percent of our offense.

This posed a real problem. Our backup tailback broke his arm during practice the previous week and wasn't even going to make the 12-hour trip with us. Johnny Teague, our young inexperienced third team freshman tailback, wasn't anywhere near ready to play. The week before, Teague was our catastrophe tailback, which meant he would only get into a game if something terrible happened to our other two players.

As soon as I learned of Pride missing the bus I figured I had better start preparing Teague to be our starter. Also, our second team fullback, Bob Crockett, was a very green freshman. I thought he should get a crash course on playing tailback just in case something happened to Teague during the game. After all, in the face of adversity, you can't just wave a white flag and surrender.

For the next three hours, Johnny Teague, Bob Crockett, and my starting quarterback, Joel McReynolds, sat in the first two rows of the bus with me. We went over our game plan for the next day. The more I drew up plays and assignments on the dry chalk board, the more a terrible feeling grew in the pit of my stomach acknowledging that Teague would not even be close to helping us win, as I had first hoped. As a matter of fact, Crockett, our backup fullback, seemed more knowledgeable about what we were doing at tailback than Teague.

Then I got a bright idea. Naturally, McReynolds, being our starting quarterback, knew exactly what everyone was supposed to do on all plays. It occurred to me that our backup quarterback, Don Mack, could help us more if he was in the game at quarterback and McReynolds was moved to tailback. Even though McReynolds had never played tailback before, he would at least provide us with a more knowledgeable player at that position. Besides, he was a tough kid and a real competitor. At the same time, I felt Mack was solid enough at quarterback to help us win the game.

I spent another two hours working with all these players, trying to get as many combinations ready as I could. Fortunately, our opponent did not field a very strong team that season. I was confident that if I could get these players to at least be sound, we could still have a chance to win the game. After all, our defense was good and we were at full strength on that side of the ball.

When the team bus finally arrived at our motel in Durango, who should I see waiting for us in the lobby but Emmett Pride. He looked scared and remorseful. Apparently he had spent the night with his girlfriend. The electricity in her apartment building had gone off which meant his alarm clock failed to wake him in time to catch the bus. Emmett knew he would be in trouble so he had his girlfriend drive the 650 miles to Durango so he could still be at the game. They made very good time and beat the bus by 45 minutes.

As I passed Emmett in the lobby, I gave him a cold stare and said loudly enough for all to hear, "You wasted your time. You're not playing tomorrow!"

You could hear a pin drop. All the players and coaches heard my verdict. Without saying anything else, I grabbed my bag and went to my room.

About a half hour later there was a knock on my door. I opened it and there stood Coach O'Connor and my three team captains. Josh Gooch, one of the captains, said, "Coach, we want to talk to you about letting Emmett play in the game tomorrow."

"No way," I replied. "You guys know the rules. Emmett missed the bus and forfeited his right to play in the game. It pisses me off that he wasn't dependable enough to make it on time."

The captains argued their case for 20 minutes claiming that Emmett was needed for us to win the game. But I refused to budge. "No way," I kept repeating.

I was a real hard ass about players being on time and being responsible. On the one hand, I wanted Emmett to play. On the other hand, I didn't want the players to think that I was soft in enforcing my rules. "We will just have to get ready to win the game without him," I said.

I did not want to cut off my nose to spite my face. I knew we would not be very good on offense if any of the other combinations I worked on during the bus trip were used, but having the players understand I was a no-nonsense coach was very important. They needed to know that breaking a rule meant living with the consequences. Even if it might mean losing a game.

Coach O'Connor sided with the captains. He recommended we punish Emmett in other ways after he played in the game. I liked that idea, but once again I was afraid that if I let him play, the other players would think winning games was more important to me than enforcing my own rules.

I stood hard on my stance, but the captains and coaches were all in favor of Emmett playing. I decided to bring the matter to a team vote. Personally, I wanted Emmett to play in the game, but I had to find a way to avoid them thinking Coach Cortese was going soft on the rules.

"Okay, I'll put it to a team vote as to whether Emmett plays or not," I said. "But I am hoping the players will respect the rules and punish him by making him sit on his ass. We'll figure out another way to win this game."

Of course I knew that throwing the decision to a team vote would almost guarantee that Emmett would play. Even though collegiate athletics is traditionally a dictatorship, there are times when you want the players to feel they have a voice in what is actually happening. If I hadn't wanted Emmett to play, he would not have. Since I wanted Emmett in the game, but did not want to appear to waiver from my position, I let democracy rule.

At our team meeting that night, I announced to the team the decision to vote on Emmett's fate. I asked Emmett to leave the room. I then addressed the team. "Men, as you know, it is a team rule that if you are late or miss events, you will be punished. Emmett Pride missed the team bus this morning and I believe he should not play in the game tomorrow. I understand that not having him on the field will make it hard for us to get the victory, but being a disciplined team is what we are all about. Doing things right all the time is more important than any one individual. I think we can still win the game without him, but since the coaches and captains are so determined to have him play and be punished in another way, I have decided to bring it to a team vote. I want to make it very clear to everyone that I am totally against him playing, but I'll leave it up to you guys."

I told them it was to be a written vote with each player getting to write down whether Emmett should play or not. Votes would be anonymous. I went up to the chalk board in the front of the room and in big letters wrote "COACH CORTESE VOTES – NOT PLAY." I then left the room and let the team go through the process.

A half hour later, Coach O'Connor came to my room and told

me the results of the team vote. The players and coaches voted 36-6 to allow him to play. Five ballots were left blank. Emmett got to play.

* * *

Postscript

We won the game 35–10. Emmett had a great day rushing the ball for 132 yards and three touchdowns. The following week I got him up at 5 a.m. six days in a row and had him jog two miles each day.

20

What's Right Is Right
– Instinct and Integrity Always Win –

In late August 1985, I received a phone call from Bob Preston, an old friend who lived in Boulder, Colorado. Preston was the assistant registrar at the University of Colorado, while I was head football coach at Mesa State College in Grand Junction.

"Bob," he began, "we've got a great athlete up here who I'm not able to enroll this fall. His name is Tony Martin and I think he's someone you might want to take a look at, in terms of your program there at Mesa State."

Bob and I were good friends while I lived in Boulder. He knew I was always looking for good players. "Sure, I'll be glad to take a look," I replied. "What's the scoop? I mean, is the kid in some kind of trouble? If he's so good, why can't you guys enroll him?"

"We found some irregularities on his application form," he said.

Uh, oh, I inwardly groaned. Irregularity was a kind of code word usually meaning "falsehood."

"As you know," Bob continued, "the University has a very strict policy concerning application form accuracy and part of my job as assistant registrar is to enforce this no-tolerance policy."

Bob proceeded to fill me in on some information about the student-athlete in question. His name was Tony Martin. He was from Miami, Florida, and had a very difficult childhood. Tony was a very special athlete who could run the 40-yard dash under 4.4 seconds—the fastest speed I had ever seen by a high school athlete. However, since Tony hadn't played during his senior year in high school, he had no scholarship to play in college. Therefore, he was attempting to enroll at the University of Colorado and try to earn a scholarship as a walk-on.

Despite Tony's great speed and athletic ability, Bob wasn't going to allow him to enroll. The football team had started practice before school officially began so Tony had been working out with the team and was doing very well at quarterback. The football team had been about two weeks into pre-season practice before Tony's application was finally evaluated for admission. The problem was discovered and subsequently, the decision was made to reject his application for admission.

Bob told me that Tony seemed like a good enough kid, but policy prevailed. He also told me that he had heard Tony had a chance to start for the Colorado Buffaloes as a freshman.

Coach Bill McCarthy was the head coach at the University of Colorado at the time. He had on his staff another old friend of mine, Gary Barnett, who later became the head coach at the University of Colorado. Gary and I went way back to our coaching days in high school. We were good friends and respected each other's coaching abilities.

After talking with Bob Preston, I decided to call Coach Barnett and get his take on the situation. Gary told me that Tony was a very special kind of athlete and that in just a few short days of practice he had shown enough ability to qualify as quarterback. He told me he was super-quick and threw the ball pretty well. I asked about his attitude and character and Gary replied that they both appeared to be very good.

Coach Barnett was very curious about my knowledge of Tony and the possibility that he might not be accepted to the University. The situation had been kept pretty quiet and was not actually known publically. He said that the football program was still working on his admission status and the final ruling had not yet been determined.

I told him that Bob Preston would make the final decision and I thought Tony's chances of being accepted weren't looking very good right now. He told me if it did not work out for Tony to enroll, he would give him my name so he could pursue coming to Mesa State College.

It was official three days later. The University of Colorado did not accept Tony. Tony then became a student at Mesa State College and was on the football field a short time later.

Tony was a great player and played two years of football for the Mesa State College Mavericks. We had many good players enrolled at Mesa State College at the time, but Tony was the final ingredient for great success.

During Tony's junior year, a situation occurred that almost cost us a chance to go to the national playoffs. Late one evening in November, I was awakened by a phone call from one of my players. I hated those late night phone calls. As a coach responsible for over 100 student-athletes, I knew that nothing good ever came from a late night phone call.

One of my players was on the other end of the line. He said that Tony Martin was being held in the city jail. I asked the reason for his arrest. The player said Tony didn't do anything wrong. *Sure*, I thought to myself, *the Grand Junction police department just goes around arresting people for no good reason.*

I grudgingly got up, dressed, and went down to the city jail to see what was happening. It was about 3 a.m. and I was very tired; we still had two games left in our regular season and we were working hard to win both of them. We felt sure if we won at least one of those final two games, we would be invited to play in the national playoffs.

Tony had posted bond by the time I arrived at the city jail and was about to leave. We went to a nearby Denny's restaurant, had a cup of coffee, and talked about what happened that evening.

Tony began by saying that he did nothing wrong and was innocent of the charge brought against him. He said he'd been at a party that evening when a fight broke out.

The girl who hosted the party was beaten up during the fight. When the police arrived, she told them Tony had started the fight and when she went to break it up he started punching her in the face. She was hurt and wanted to press charges against Tony for assault. Tony went on to say that when the fight started, he and a couple of his friends left the party fearing that trouble was brewing. A short time later he was picked up by the police and charged with assault. He denied ever punching her and claimed he did not know who did.

I had a problem. As a head college coach, I had the responsibility of recruiting players of good character into our program. When trouble occurs within a team, coaches must deal with it fairly and with integrity. Sometimes that means cutting loose the culprits who cause problems. My real problem was if I played Tony the following week while he still had the charge of assault against him, it would seem as if I wasn't concerned about anything other than winning football games. His court date was set for 40 days after the incident, which meant he would not get to play the rest of the season. If he didn't play the rest of the season, he would have been punished whether or not he was guilty of any crime.

Tony was a great player and the NFL was interested in him as a possible player. By not getting to play the final two games of the regular season and any playoff games, his future would be jeopardized since it would appear that we were condemning his integrity and honesty.

I knew two things. One, Tony did not drink or use drugs. He was always concerned about keeping his body in top condition and was not about to drink alcohol or use drugs. And secondly, I had never caught Tony lying to me about anything.

I wanted to talk to the girl who pressed the charges to see what she had to say about the incident. I already had Tony's statement, but I wanted to get her version of the events that transpired that night.

One of her parents answered the phone. I learned that she was a resident of Grand Junction and enrolled at Mesa State. I assured the girl and her parents that I wasn't going to badger her or try to get her to change her story. I just wanted to hear her side of what happened that night.

The girl came to my office the following day with one of her friends. She told me the same story she had told the police and she had the bruises on her face to prove it. I told her Tony denied that he ever hit her and I asked if she was sure it was Tony. She said she was.

I was perplexed. On the one hand I had this girl identifying Tony as the guy who beat her up. And on the other hand, I had Tony - who I had no reason to doubt - telling me he was innocent.

Fortunately, I knew someone who was also at the party that evening and could provide an independent source of information, a young man named Johnny Pagano. (I write about Johnny in another chapter.) Johnny's mother and father were personal friends I had known virtually all his life; indeed, Johnny was like a relative and I trusted him very much. Even though Johnny and Tony were friends as well as teammates, I was confident that Johnny wouldn't lie to me if I asked him what really happened.

Johnny told me he was in another room of the house when the fight broke out and he did not see the girl get hit in the face. He did say, however, that he didn't think Tony could have been involved with the ruckus because he was dancing with someone else at that time and he thought both of them ran into the room where the fight broke out at the same time. I asked him if he knew who punched the girl. He stammered for a bit then finally said he thought he knew who it was. Although he didn't actually see it himself, he heard it was a former player who also was in attendance at the party.

Now I felt more confused than ever. The local newspaper ran an article discussing whether Tony should be allowed to play in any games until the case had been settled. The court date was not going to take place until after the playoffs. What should a coach do?

I decided to call an old friend, Terry Ferina, and seek his counsel. Terry was the previous district attorney in Grand Junction and was now a very successful and respected community leader. I told him the situation and asked his advice. He responded by saying he wanted to talk to his successor, the new district attorney, and that he would get back to me ASAP.

Terry called back within a few hours and told me the DA's office was planning to pursue the case against Tony Martin. They told Terry that all the evidence and interviews pointed to Tony as being the attacker.

"Now what?" I asked.

Terry wanted to know what Tony had told me. I said Tony denied ever hitting anyone at the party. Terry then reminded me of a very basic American legal premise: *A person is presumed innocent until proven guilty.* If I were to keep Tony from playing the last two games of the season, I would have prejudged his innocence or guilt. Hence, despite whatever negative publicity it might generate, Tony had a right to his day in court as well as his time on the field.

Without actually telling me to play Tony, Terry made me feel I had no right to presume his guilt and punish him. I decided to let Tony play in the up-coming games and took the resulting community criticism from some who disagreed with my decision. It should be understood that I did not allow Tony to play because I wanted to win; I allowed him to play because it was the right thing to do.

We probably would have won the last two games of the regular season even without Tony at quarterback. Tony played those two games because I believed in my heart he was innocent.

* * *

Postscript

Tony Martin was found innocent when the case went to trial several weeks later. Apparently, the girl who brought charges against him was drunk that night and was mistaken in identifying who actually attacked her. It was also brought to the court's attention that her girlfriend, who was in attendance at the time of the fight, had asked Tony out a week before and he turned her down.

Tony Martin went on to the National Football League and played 13 years as a wide receiver. He was All-Pro and played in one Super Bowl.

Section II

Playing Years: The Good, the Bad and the Awkward

21

The Perils of Misperception
— *Union Negotiations Fall Short* —

Saturday November 2, 1963. "Hey Leon, there's Bud Wilkinson!" I whispered in awe to my friend and teammate Leon Mavity, as the legendary football coach walked onto Owen Field in Norman, Oklahoma.

I was a junior linebacker at the University of Colorado and we were going through warm-ups and stretching exercises prior to the game. This was my first game in Oklahoma, my first time playing in front of 50,000 fans, and my first time to see Master Coach Bud Wilkinson in person. This would also be the first match-up between a master and his disciple. Eddie Crowder, Colorado's first-year head coach, had both played for Wilkinson and served as an assistant coach on Wilkinson's staff.

Colorado was not a very good football team that season. Oklahoma was a good deal better. Nevertheless, we worked hard and Coach Crowder did a good job of cranking us up for the return to his alma mater. Coach convinced us that if we played hard and made no mistakes, we could win.

The Buffaloes' warm-up area was the south end zone. My dream was about to come true. I had always wanted to play college football at its highest level. This was it. I remember "goose-necking" around and thinking that I had finally made it to the big time! Even though I knew I wasn't likely to get much playing time that day, I still felt very excited and giddy.

The coaches had us do a one-on-one blocking drill. This drill called for the offensive and defensive linemen to form two lines facing each other. One by one we would try to block each other as the coaches tried to motivate each of us. Naturally, the coaches always wanted the players to go full-speed against each other. They tried to get us to knock the crap out of one another even during meaningless warm-up drills.

During those days, the players formed what we called a "union." The union was organized by the players to make things easier and to protect each other from showing up one another just during warm-ups. We learned how to make it appear that we were going hard and full-speed; but in fact, each player would just grunt and growl to make it look good. By doing this, nobody would win or lose and each player could get out of the drill with a whole skin and still be in good graces with the coach. This charade could be the reason we only won two games that season.

Not every player on our team participated in the union. Some were always going to try hard to impress the coaches. Therefore, it was important to know which players were union members and which were not. You never wanted to get in a situation where your opponent was going full-speed and you weren't.

Jerry McClurg was our team's biggest and best lineman. He was also one of the founders of the union. Jerry came from Grand Junction, Colorado, and became one of my best friends. As I approached the front of the one-on-one line during warm-ups that afternoon, I noticed I was going to go up against Jerry. Since Jerry was a good union member I thought there would be no problem. Both of us would just follow the usual union technique and move on. I looked at Jerry. He was standing in the line across from me. I gave him the union nod, meaning, *Let's just go through the motions and let the coaches think we are working really hard.* As I nodded, Jerry seemed to nod back to me. I thought maybe he might be overdoing his nodding a bit, but I figured he wanted to make sure I got the message.

It was now our turn to go against one another. Coaches Rudy Feldman and Joe Harper were screaming for us to get after it. Here we were, probably five minutes away from playing the Sooners and they wanted us jacked up. Both of them sure were!

I got down into my defensive stance, Jerry's head nodded slightly as he got ready to block me. I thought he was really overdoing the union signal. Since I was on defense, I waited for Jerry to make the first move. As he fired out towards me, I started to lunge into him. Keep in mind, Jerry was a real load. Not only was he big, but he was also strong and very quick. On my best day going full-speed against Jerry, I would struggle to win any battle. I was traveling a little more than half-speed, as a good union member should, when this huge man unloaded on me.

He hit me with such force that my head snapped back and my knees buckled. As he pinned me to the ground, the coaches and other sideliners went crazy. It was such a vicious hit that it got everyone fired up. Coaches Harper and Feldman rushed out to congratulate Jerry for making such a devastating block. There I was, lying flat on my back, trying to figure out what had just happened. Both coaches actually stepped on my surprised and embarrassed body in their rush to get to Jerry.

All coaches like to finish pre-game drills on a strong note. Jerry McClurg's block on me had fired up the whole team. As if on cue, the band started playing the national anthem. Everyone started running to the sidelines for the anthem. As I got slowly to my feet and tried to clear the fog from my brain, Jerry came back to help me up. I was pissed. "What the fuck were you doing?" I screamed at him. "I gave you the union nod and you returned it; and the next thing I know you're going full-speed. That's bullshit, Jerry!"

"No, no," he stammered. "I was trying to signal you that the union was off. Coach Crowder came up to me as I was standing in line and told me if I won the battle against you in the drill, he would start me and make me a team captain today. I tried to signal that the union was off!"

* * *

Postscript

We lost the game 35-0. Bud Wilkinson really must have had strong feelings for his former disciple, Coach Crowder, because Wilkinson's Sooners probably could have rolled up an additional 50 points that afternoon. I was so mad at Jerry that I didn't talk to him for three or four days.

22

Alumni Adrenaline
– The Reality of Age –

It's hard to give up something you love – particularly when that something is a sport you've been playing most of your life. It was that way with me and football.

Nineteen-sixty-four was my final year of eligibility at the University of Colorado. Following two failed attempts to play pro ball for the now defunct American Football League, I sadly recognized that my playing days were over. I can't explain it, but I felt that I had just lost a good friend.

Fortunately for me, coaching soon filled that void. Coach Eddie Crowder, head coach at the University of Colorado at the time, hired me to work as a student assistant. My job was to work with Coach Dan Stavely who coached the freshmen.

During this period, the University of Colorado played an annual spring football game against an alumni team. After the varsity finished 20 days of spring football practice, the alumni would be invited back to play against the varsity. The old vets would return to campus, practice for two days, drink for two nights, and try to beat the varsity on a Saturday afternoon. Naturally, I saw this as a chance for me to suit up and play again, so I always participated.

I played in the first 14 alumni games. It was great fun coming back to Boulder, seeing old team mates and reconnecting with the football program. Now stop and think about a guy playing in only one game a year, for 14 straight years, with just two practices before each game. Probably not the wisest strategy for a 35-year-old. After the ninth spring game, I was asked to be a player-coach and help get the alumni ready for their yearly "battle royale."

In 1979, I was assistant football coach at Colorado under Head Coach Bill Mallory. He continued the tradition of the alumni games when he replaced Coach Crowder. Since I had played in each of the previous 14 alumni games and helped organize their programs, Coach Mallory released me from my team coaching duties for two days so I could coach the alumni. His passed on some words of advice. "Just coach, don't try to play in the game. Our varsity players would kill an old man like you," he cautioned.

Initially, I planned to follow Mallory's advice and just coach the alumni. However, as we got closer to game time, we realized that we did not have an alumni center returning for this game. This created a problem. How could we have an alumni game without a returning player at center?

Fred Cassoti, long-time assistant athletic director, asked me to suit up one more time and play center. He realized it wouldn't be much of a game without at least one alumnus returning as center. I agreed. This meant I could still keep my personal streak alive of playing in all 14 games. Knowing I no longer had the capability of playing very many plays, I asked Coach Mallory if we could use two freshmen centers from the varsity to help fill the void. The plan was for me to start the game, play a few series, and then let the freshmen finish it out. Mallory agreed, but again reminded me that I shouldn't even try to play at all.

"Bob, you're crazy to think you can play center. Do you know who our nose guard is?" he chuckled.

"Yes, I know who the nose guard is," I replied. Lavall Short was our starting nose guard, which meant he would line up on the center for the entire game. He was a pre-season All Big Eight candidate and one of our top returning players. Standing 6'2" and a very solid 284 pounds, he was one of the strongest players on the varsity. By way of comparison, I stood 5'11" and weighed 220 pounds of pure flab. Talk about a mismatch!

Silly me. I thought I could do a decent job against Lavall. After all, I was still competitive and surely I could play maybe half of a quarter – possibly 10 to 14 plays – and still hold my own against Lavall. Remember, as an assistant coach with the varsity, I got to observe Lavall manhandle our offensive center daily. Little did I know that my tough-guy attitude would soon get my weak body into trouble.

George Belu, the offensive coordinator and a dear friend, was a jokester deluxe. He was always pulling pranks or saying something that would off-set the monotony of practicing football. He thought I was crazy to attempt playing against the varsity.

The plan was that I would start the game, play as long as I could, then let the youngsters take over. I was by far the oldest returning alumnus to start the game and that made me feel very macho. I remember overhearing my two teenage sons brag to their friends that their dad was going to start in the alumni game. That felt good.

Before the game started, each alumnus was introduced over the loud speaker in the stadium. Each player would jog from the end zone to the middle of the field when his name and number were called. When my name was called, the announcer also included that I was a second team All Big Eight center in 1965.

Wait a minute, I thought to myself. *I was never even a starter until my senior year and even then I didn't start every game.* I never earned Big Eight recognition for my unspectacular career at Colorado. But when I returned to play in the alumni games, the announcer always padded my playing career more generously than the pads I wore. The first few years I played in the game, I was introduced as the starting center my senior season. The third and fourth time I returned, I was introduced as a three-year starter at center. By the sixth alumni game I was introduced as a captain of the 1966 team. Not true. By my 10th return, I was an honorable mention All Big Eight center. Now, in my 14th game, I was introduced as a second team All Big Eight player. Wow, if only I could have played in a few more alumni games, I would have made All-American!

Back to the alumni game. As I was getting dressed in the locker room, Coach Belu came in and yelled out, "Where is big, bad Bob Cortese?" As he wandered over to where I was putting on my uniform, he said, "Coach Mallory wanted me to give you something to keep with you at all times this afternoon." He picked up my helmet, pulled out an oral screw from his back pocket, and tied the device to my face mask, amidst a great deal of locker room laughter. (An oral screw is a device that doctors and trainers keep in their medicine kits to prevent players from swallowing their tongues while unconscious.)

"You know Lavall is going to eat your lunch today," Belu said, as I put on my helmet with the oral screw now dangling from my face mask. The laughter continued.

The varsity kicked off to the alumni and we took over the ball on our own 18-yard line. Our starting quarterback was Bernie McCall. Bernie was a good friend and decent quarterback on some very average teams. He was a real joker and would always try to pull the wool over someone's eyes.

Our first play was a dive off right tackle. As we broke the huddle, I ran up to the line of scrimmage and low and behold there was Lavall Short waiting for me to snap the ball. It was amazing how big he looked and how small I felt. I had coached this guy for two years and he never looked as big as he did at that moment. The play was going to be snapped on the second count. As Bernie got under my butt, I heard Lavall sing, "Good afternoon, Coach Cortese."

Trying to be macho and sound like I was a tough guy, I responded, "Screw you, Lavall." I then snapped the ball and before I could fire out and get a block on the beast, he slid to my right and hit the ball carrier before he could get back to the line of scrimmage.

The next play was a sweep once again going to our right. After I snapped the ball, Lavall read the play and ran the halfback down for another loss of yardage before I could even get a hit on him. Back in the huddle the players were screaming at me to at least slow Lavall down so we could have a chance to run a play.

I felt very inadequate and decided I was just going to tackle Lavall. After all, what official would call an old coach for holding in an alumni game? Approaching the line of scrimmage, I once again set my hands on the ball, and while looking into my large opponent's eyes, I knew I had to do something to slow him down. I was determined to tackle him to the ground so Bernie could pass the football downfield.

As I snapped the ball to Bernie, I reached out to grab Lavall and tried to take him to the ground. No such luck. When the young stud saw Bernie drop back to pass the ball, he threw his right forearm into my chest and tossed me to the ground instead. I was no match for him. He sacked Bernie five yards deep in our own backfield.

I went back to help Bernie up from the ground, as all good offensive linemen do when they whiff on a defender. Bernie just stared at me and with a tentative smile on his face said, "Shit, I think he broke my leg."

I reached out with my hand to pull him up saying, "Cut out

screwing around and get up."

Bernie was always kidding around. "No, seriously, I think he broke my leg," he said.

I helped pull him to his feet and we both stumbled off the field together. Bernie limped considerably. The team doctor met us on the sideline. He took one look at Bernie's leg and pronounced, "It's broken."

I felt terrible and realized that I had no business being out on the field at the age of 35. I went over to the two freshman centers we had recruited from the varsity and told them to finish playing the game.

I took off my helmet and shoulder pads for the final time.

*   *   *

Postscript

I continued coaching the alumni for five more years. I never suited up again. Bernie McCall and I remain friends.

23

Redshirt Surprise

– Practice Makes Perfect –

As long as I can remember, I have wanted to be a football coach. When I was a high school player at St. Aquinas High School in Rochester, New York, I would evaluate all the coaches I played under. If one of them did something I didn't think was effective, I'd tell myself, *I'll never do that when I am a coach.* I'd also make notes on the effective techniques those coaches used to motivate me. Throughout the following years, while playing at the University of Colorado, my goal to be a coach never wavered.

When my football eligibility at Colorado ran out at the end of 1964, I still needed another year-and-a-half of course work before I could graduate. Head Coach Eddie Crowder came to my rescue. He graciously kept me on scholarship for the extra time I needed to earn my degree. Coach Crowder allowed me to become a student coach and work directly under defensive coordinator Rudy Feldman. Coach Feldman was also very good to me. He taught me a great deal about football and, in particular, scouting opponents.

They anointed me as the "redshirt" coach. As such, I was responsible for handling 33 players who were being redshirted that year. (A redshirted player is one who practices with the team but does not play in any games, thus allowing him to retain a full year of eligibility.) Many coaches use redshirts as practice fodder. Since they can't play intercollegiate games, they become lost souls to the varsity coaches and are virtually ignored. Mainly, redshirts function as scout team players, in which they help the varsity players by running plays and simulating the upcoming opponents.

As the redshirt coach, I was responsible for viewing game films and charting our opponent's offensive plays each week. With the help of Coach Feldman, I would draw the plays they would run on eight-by-eleven cards. I'd make sure each player's position was drawn on the card so that the scout team could simulate what we thought our weekly opponent might do against us.

Because they didn't play in games, redshirts were seldom taught what plays our team was actually running. Coaches spent almost all of their time working with players who would actually be playing. The redshirts never got to work on any one offense, but instead they did just what the scouting cards directed.

Each week, Colorado would play a different team with a different offense. Wing T, Power I, and Split-Back formation were just a few of the systems we faced during the season. As a young coach, I learned a lot.

One Wednesday during the 1965 season, Coach Crowder called me into his office. He told me that after the varsity left for its game vs. Missouri on Friday, we were going to let the redshirts play a game against the freshmen. (That was back in the days before the NCAA passed the *freshmen eligibility* rule.)

Our freshmen team was coached by Dan Stavely along with some other graduate assistants. They practiced and played a couple of games a year against some other college freshmen teams in the area. Since their practice field was a different field from what the varsity used, they rarely had much contact with the varsity. As a result of having their own practices, the freshmen developed more as a team than the older, but less-organized, redshirts.

Coach Crowder wanted me to work the redshirts so that they could at least line up and give the freshmen a good effort. When I asked him what plays he wanted me to use in this scrimmage game, he said that he didn't care. He explained that since the redshirts never worked on any one particular offense, he just wanted them to put a few plays together so that the freshmen would get some good work. He told me the scrimmage was for the benefit of the freshmen and I should not to be disappointed when they won.

Crowder also noted that the freshmen class was loaded with many future stars, and despite being younger, they would probably trounce the redshirts.

Bullshit, I said to myself.

After practice on Thursday, I held a redshirts-only meeting. I told the guys about the plan to scrimmage the talented freshmen team two days later. Not surprisingly, they were excited to be put into a real game situation. They were not sure what offense we were going to run, but they did feel good that they were finally going to play a somewhat real game.

I told them what Coach Crowder had said about not expecting too much as we would probably lose to the freshmen. "Bullshit!" I said. "We are going to beat the crap out of those young *prima donnas.*"

"What plays are we going to run?" asked Dave Sidwell, one of the older redshirts.

"Missouri's plays," I told him. Since we had spent an entire week running Missouri's offense against the varsity in preparation for their upcoming battle this weekend, I thought we should be in pretty good shape to run those same plays against our freshmen.

"We don't know their assignments," said another redshirt, "and two days is an awfully short time to learn them."

"We'll run the cards in and out of the huddle, just as we do when we work against the varsity," I replied. "Instead of my holding the cards and showing you what your assignments are, we'll shuffle the cards in and out with each play. The quarterback will show it to the team in the huddle, break the huddle and execute the play." I thought we might need an extra practice or two in order to get more organized, so I went to the intramural department and asked the director if he would leave the lights on their fields after they were finished playing intramural games that evening. He agreed.

I then went to Coach Stavely and asked, "Instead of playing the game on Friday afternoon, could we postpone it until Saturday morning?" I told him the extra day would enable me to better prepare the redshirts, and this, in turn, would give the freshmen a better effort. Stavely, like Coach Crowder, never imagined the redshirts could get organized enough to compete with his talented group of young players. He thought moving the game to Saturday was a good idea because it would give some of the local freshmen a better chance to get their families and friends in the stands.

Nobody, and I do mean nobody, with the exception of the 33 redshirts and two student coaches (Walt Klinker and me) thought there was the remotest of possibilities that the freshmen team would lose.

After Thursday's practice, we met as a team and started to get organized. We wanted to keep these plans secret and not let anyone know how much we were going to prepare for the scrimmage. At 9:30 that evening, we held a spirited hour-and-a-half practice. The redshirts loved it. For the first time in quite a while, these players were working for a game and were therefore highly motivated to practice.

Since the varsity was gone on Friday, we practiced for another hour-and-a-half that afternoon. Once again we met that evening and put the final touches on our game plan for the following morning. What fun it was to watch these gladiators prepare for a game that meant absolutely nothing to anyone but us!

I called five high school football officials and asked them to referee the game. I also recruited a chain crew from the intramural department to work the sidelines for the game/scrimmage. I met with Fred Cassotti, the assistant athletic director, and asked if we could use the scoreboard for the scrimmage. He agreed with the qualification that it was okay with Coach Crowder.

Following his conversation with Mr. Cassotti, Coach Crowder called me to say that he was glad I was organizing the scrimmage. He re-emphasized that the chances of the talented and well-organized freshmen team losing to a group of rag-tag redshirts – a motley bunch who never practiced any schemes or systems – was highly unlikely. Clearly, Coach Crowder didn't want me to be disappointed with the outcome.

"I understand, Coach," I assured him.

Game day. Coach Klinker and I had breakfast with the redshirts in the dorm. Then we marched *en masse* to Folsom Stadium where we entered the locker room and got ready for the game. The freshmen were as excited as we were. The two teams warmed up in different ends of the stadium. The game attracted about 300 interested spectators. Even the local Boulder newspaper sent a reporter to cover the game.

As planned, the redshirts ran plays from the same cards as the Missouri plays they ran against the varsity all week long. I would select a play and send it onto the field with a substitute wide receiver. He would then hold the card up so all the players in the huddle could see what their assignments were. The other wide receiver would then run the card off the field and the redshirts would execute that play.

The system worked surprisingly well. The redshirts executed their assignments with precision. After all, they were used to running plays from scouting cards, because that's all they had been doing all season long.

Final score: redshirts 21; freshmen 14. We won! We won! We won!

My redshirts erupted with yelling, screaming and great enthusiasm. Three players grabbed me and hoisted me onto their shoulders. As they carried me off the field, I remember thinking, *Coaching is great! This is what I want to do for the rest of my life.*

The next Monday afternoon I ran across Bob Anderson, the high school All-American quarterback from Boulder High School, who was now the starting quarterback for the freshmen team. "Coach Cortese, your boys did a great job on Saturday. I have to take my hat off to you for getting them ready." Coach Crowder called to congratulate me and the redshirts for doing such a good job. He told me that running the cards from that week's practice was pretty smart.

* * *

Postscript

The only real fun in playing football is in playing actual games. Unlike many other sports, football practice is not fun. Basketball is fun to practice. Shooting baskets is fun. That is why you see so many baskets in driveways throughout the country. How many kids do you ever see in their front yards working on tackling and blocking?

24

Seeing Stars

— A Celestial Day in Stillwater –

It happened on a Monday in October 1964. The University of Colorado football locker room was decked out with all kinds of information about our next opponent, Oklahoma State University. As I walked into the training room, I noticed one particular article posted on the bulletin board for all to see. I am not sure if the article was from a newspaper or *Sports Illustrated* magazine, but it was enlarged and highlighted. The article featured Walt Garrison, the great running back for OSU.

As a linebacker for the Buffs, I was particularly interested to read what was being said about our next opponent's superstar running back. The article was lengthy, but one specific part jumped out at me. In his three-year college football career, Garrison had never been stopped for a loss. Now that impressed me. Here was a guy who carried the ball 25 to 30 times a game and no one ever tackled him behind the line of scrimmage.

Garrison was from Lewisville, Texas, and always wore a cowboy hat, cowboy boots, jeans and most of the time had a wad of chewing tobacco stuffed in his lower jaw. It's hard to say whether he was a tough cowboy who happened to play football or a football player who happened to be a cowboy. He obviously loved both football and the rodeo. He was a standout in both sports. During football season, he played fullback for the Oklahoma State Cowboys; and during the off-season, he traveled the rodeo circuit as a steer wrestler and bull rider.

One of the things I noticed about Garrison as I viewed game films in preparation for this week's game was that he was a "north-south" runner; that is, 95 percent of the time he ran plays straight up the middle. Dives, slants, and traps were his specialties. Even when he was moved from his customary fullback position to half-back, he still went straight ahead. He ran low and he ran hard. He was very good at breaking tackles and moving the piles. He was rarely taken to the ground by just one man.

We arrived in Stillwater, Oklahoma, fired-up and ready to play. Neither CU nor OSU was a powerhouse in the Big Eight Conference at that time, so each team thought they could and should win the game. In the middle of the second quarter, our coaches called for a blitz. As right-side linebacker, my assignment was to shoot the gap between their center and guard. Garrison was lined up at the fullback position.

I timed my blitz perfectly. As the ball was snapped, I got into the gap before OSU's guard was able to block me. The quarterback turned and pitched the ball to Garrison, who, to my surprise, start-ed to sweep away from me. (The surprise was because Garrison sel-dom ran east and west.) I got about two yards into their backfield when the story about Garrison never having been thrown for a loss flashed into my mind. I found myself unblocked and deep in the enemy backfield with the "great" Walt Garrison running parallel to the line of scrimmage. *Here is my chance to be a hero*, I thought. It's amazing what one can think of in just a few short moments. *I can be the first player to tackle this future All-American for a loss,*

I fantasized.

As I closed in for the kill, Garrison glanced my way and then suddenly planted his right foot into the ground and changed direction. Instead of running laterally, he was now lowering his shoulder and driving straight towards me. We were both still a couple of yards deep in the backfield when the collision took place. WHACK! I felt like I had just been hit by one of those 2,500 pound bulls Garrison rode in the rodeo arena. I hung on for dear life and it was obvious that there was no way I was going to take this man down.

Not only did Garrison break my tackle, but he went on to gain three yards on the play. I saw little lights blinking on and off above my eyes. As I got up from the ground, I understood what people meant when they said they "see stars" after a collision. That was as hard a hit as I have ever taken.

* * *

Postscript

Oklahoma State beat us that afternoon 14-10. Garrison led the Big Eight in rushing that season and in 1966 was drafted by the Dallas Cowboys where he played nine seasons, making the Pro Bowl team once.

25

Tunnel Vision

– A Memorable Grand Entrance –

"Okay men, if we can contain Mike Garrett and not give Craig Fertig time to throw the ball downfield, then we will win tomorrow's game." It was Friday, September 14, and University of Colorado Buffaloes' (CU) Coach Eddie Crowder was giving us final instructions before the next day's season-opening game against the defending 1964 Rose Bowl champions, the Trojans from the University of Southern California (USC). The game would be played in the famed Los Angeles Coliseum, site of the 1932 Olympics.

"Let's go to our rooms, get a good night's sleep, and be ready to beat the Trojans!"

Crowder really had us pumped up.

The meeting broke up and we started toward our assigned rooms. Coach Rudy Feldman, defensive coordinator for the Buffaloes, asked us to stop. "Listen up men," he bellowed. "Tomorrow when we break out of the locker room and run down the tunnel into the Coliseum, be careful. The tunnel to the field is steep and very slippery. I have seen many players fly down that slick concrete runway and slide on their asses right onto the field. Some players have even been hurt doing so."

Coach Feldman played at UCLA so he had a few occasions to run down onto that field himself. "Remember to control your emotions and walk carefully down to the field," he warned. "After we get on the grass, then we can sprint across the field to our sidelines." Then he looked right at my roommate John (Jet) Marchiol and said, "Do you hear me, John? I don't want to see someone from Trinidad, Colorado, embarrassing himself or the team by sliding on his ass onto the field." That provoked a round of laughter, at John's expense, of course, and we continued on to our rooms.

John seemed upset when we got to our room. "What's up, Jet?" I asked.

"Why does Coach Feldman always have to pick on me?" he complained. "It just pisses me off that he has to use me as his goat every time he wants to get a laugh."

I smiled and told him, "Forget about it and try not to be so sensitive." In an effort to get John's mind off being singled out by the coach, I started talking about the tunnel situation. "Wouldn't it be the shits if you were the guy to get hurt running down that ramp onto the field?" I joked. John didn't think it was funny.

Game day came. On my way into the locker room, I noticed what Coach Feldman had mentioned - the tunnel walkway leading to the field did appear to be very slick. Contributing to the danger of losing my footing was the type of football shoes players wore back then - nylon cleats an inch long with metal tips. Talk about being slick! Coach Feldman wasn't kidding when he said it was like walking on ice. You could do it but you had better be careful.

Two minutes before our time to leave the locker room, the Trojan football players began banging on the wall that separated their locker room from ours. "BUFFALO MEAT! BUFFALO MEAT!" We could hear them chant as they banged on the wall. A little intimidating. Legendary coach John McKay may have had his USC team playing as well as any in the U.S. that season, but I was damn sure I wasn't going to let those "west coast surfers" intimidate me.

As we were preparing to leave the locker room and walk down the dreaded tunnel to the field, one of the coaches reminded us again to walk cautiously and not run until we hit the field.

My tradition was to be the last player to leave the locker room before we entered the field for battle. Maybe I did this because I was waiting until the last minute to decide whether I wanted to go or not, or maybe I thought being at the end of the line entering the field might keep me from being pelted by flying objects that some of the fans might throw at the enemy. Whatever, I just liked being the last one out to the field.

"BUFFALO MEAT! BUFFALO MEAT!" continued the chant from the Trojan locker room. Trying to act like a tough guy I yelled for all to hear, "Screw those bastards; let's go out there and kick some ass!"

As was my tradition, I waited behind as our team started making their way to the field. All of us were walking ever-so-cautiously down the slippery tunnel to the field below. Bringing up the rear, I was particularly careful walking down.

As I got halfway through the tunnel, I heard USC still chanting and getting ready to follow us down. Both teams were required to be on the field for the national anthem. *Clippety-clap, clippety-clap.* I could hear the Trojans coming from behind me. I thought it was unusual for them to be coming down so much faster then we had, but I thought maybe they were wearing a different type of shoe, which explained the strange and repetitious sounds which seemed to be approaching me from behind. *Clippety-clap, clippety-clap.* They seemed to be getting closer and closer. I could see my teammates turning and looking back and starting to move to the side. *Bullshit,* I said to myself, *I am not looking back or moving out of the way for those jerks!*

Clippety-clap, clippety-clap. They seemed to be getting closer and closer. I was determined not to look back or step aside as my "sissy" teammates were doing.

Clippety-clap, clippety-clap. I was sure they were about to run right over me. I finally turned around to see what was happening. To my surprise, there was a crazy guy dressed in a Trojan uniform, waving a sword, riding a white stallion, and galloping down the tunnel to make his grand entrance into the Coliseum. As the horse gained on me, I slipped on the ramp and fell on the hard and slippery concrete surface. SWOOOOOSH. There I went, sliding down the tunnel right onto the playing field.

What a grand entrance! In front of 50,000 fans! When I finally got to my feet I felt a stabbing pain in my butt. People rushed up to see if I was okay. I was way too embarrassed to tell them my ass hurt but I think to this day that damned Trojan horse stepped on me as I was sliding down the ramp into the Coliseum.

*   *   *

Postscript

We lost the game 21-0 and I still believe that damned white horse stepped on me so I couldn't play at full strength.

26

Underestimating an Opponent
– Gale Who? –

Our game plan was very simple: *Stop Gale Sayers!* I was a junior center/linebacker at the University of Colorado; Gale Sayers was a senior running back for the University of Kansas.

We were preparing for our away game with Coach Rudy Feldman as our defensive coordinator. Coach Feldman made it very clear that Sayers was the key to Kansas's success.

During our team meeting on the Sunday before the game, Coach Feldman emphasized this by saying, "Men, if we're going to win this week we have to stop their All-American running back, Gale Sayers. He's not only fast, but very elusive and tough." Feldman then ran a highlight film of about 20 plays showing Sayers running over, around, and through his previous opponents.

Colorado's defense at the time was known as an "OKIE 5-2." Coach Feldman's plan was to have both linebackers key every move that Sayers made during the game. Previously when we played a team that had a good runner in the offensive backfield, we would assign one linebacker to mirror his every move. Since Sayers was considered so extraordinary, Coach felt we needed both backers just watching him. As players, we were unsure why one player warranted so much attention. Even after watching the highlight film, we were not convinced anyone could be that good.

After a spirited week of practice with the coaches relentlessly intimidating us about Sayers's invincibility, we arrived in Lawrence and were ready for battle. Before the kickoff I remember telling Steve Sidwell (another Colorado linebacker) that we were probably making a big mistake by having so many people focusing on Sayers. (You see, even back then I thought I was a coach.)

I was on the coverage team for the opening kickoff, playing one player in from the right side. Sayers was on the return team. I remember him circling under the kickoff and I fervently hoped that he would come my way so I could nail him and show those coaches that Sayers was not all that big of a deal. My wish was granted as the great Sayers sprinted to my side of the field. I was careful not to let him get outside of me. I broke towards him trying to keep him aligned on my inside shoulder. I ran past a Kansas blocker who was probably assigned to block me, thinking that my opportunity had arrived. I knew that Sayers saw me coming towards him. He first made a move upfield, then suddenly broke to my outside. As I tried to adjust to his two quick moves, I started to lose my balance. Trying to stay on my feet, I broke back to the outside to cut him off. As I did that, he made another quick move darting back across the field. I tried to cut back after him, but again, his moves were too quick and sharp. I felt like a bull in a china shop on a newly-waxed floor.

I couldn't keep up with him as he started going back to the other side of the field. I stumbled and went to the ground. As I started to get up from the ground, the All-American had already reversed the field, put a move on one of my teammates who was playing on the other side, and was starting back towards me. He had made the same move on my teammate as he did to me, plus faking and jerking him to the ground. Just as I was recovering from his moves to my side of the field, I turned and he ran smack into me. I never saw him coming and I'm sure he never saw me.

At the time, I wasn't quite sure what had happened. I thought someone blocked me. Over on Colorado's bench, my teammates and coaches were all screaming and yelling, "GREAT HIT! GOOD JOB!"

I trotted over to the sideline, still not knowing what actually had happened on the field. Coach Feldman came over to me, patted my helmet, and said, "Great tackle, that's how to start a ball game!" I assumed I had done something good.

Sayers had a hard time running the ball against us that afternoon. Every time he made a move, our entire defense would swarm all over him. Another Kansas back (someone we had never even heard about from our coaches) however, had a big game and they beat us 10-7.

* * *

Postscript

Throughout my 38 years of coaching, I have said and done some stupid things. None, however, more wrong than after that game. While we were flying back to Boulder, Colorado, I turned to my teammate, John Marchiol, and said, "You know, that Sayers guy is never going to make it in the NFL. He's way overrated."

27

Best Efforts Not Always Enough
– Offsides vs. Oklahoma –

"McQuarters will kick your ass all the way back to New York!" Coach Eddie Crowder screamed at me because I wasn't practicing with the intensity he wanted to see. Coach was furious at me. He expected his players to practice at the same high level of intensity as they used in the game. In his view, I lacked heart. I was a junior at the University of Colorado and Coach Crowder was our head coach.

We were getting ready to play the University of Oklahoma. Crowder was both a former player and assistant coach for the Sooners; he knew how good Ed McQuarters really was. Crowder had recruited and coached the big defensive lineman from Tulsa before taking the head coaching job at the University of Colorado. This was Coach Crowder's second year at CU and he wanted nothing more than to upset his alma mater.

We were running through some blocking drills and I was going about three-quarter speed from my offensive guard position. Coach Crowder could see that I wasn't going all-out and he was not happy. As he ran screaming towards me, he threw his baseball cap. The cap sailed towards me and the sharp-edged bill somehow jabbed through my face mask, cutting me under my right eye. The days of players wearing those big cages had not yet arrived, making it possible for flying objects to come close.

Despite my bleeding, Coach kept yelling about what a stud McQuarters was and how he would dominate me when I would try to block him. Even after the trainer came over and was patching up the small cut, Coach continued, "McQuarters is big and strong. He will be the best you are going to go up against this season. There is no way you will handle him with the minimal effort you're demonstrating today."

Years later, when I was a graduate assistant working under Coach Crowder, I learned his strategy for game-week practice. Early in the week you push your team hard. You get their attention and respect for the upcoming opponent by threatening and making them believe the other team is very good and chances to beat them very slim. As the week progresses, you gradually build your team's confidence. The day before the game, you brag about their readiness and likelihood of winning, assuming they stay focused.

Game day finally arrived: September 7, 1964. The University of Oklahoma vs. the University of Colorado at Folsom Field in Boulder, Colorado.

Back in those days, players had to play both offense and defense. You could only substitute one player per play and that was how we would get plays called from the bench. I was one of the messenger guards. Dick Mankowski and I would alternate plays at the guard position. The coaches would send one of us into the game relaying to the quarterback what play they wanted us to run.

Gomer Jones was in his first year as head coach for the University of Oklahoma, succeeding Hall of Fame Coach Bud Wilkinson. In our second possession in the first quarter, we marched the ball down to the Oklahoma 12-yard line. We had a third down and two. Our fans were ecstatic. As Mankowski came off the field, Coach

Crowder grabbed me by the shoulder pads, looked me straight in the eyes and said, "Listen to me carefully. I want to run 22 dive, but tell Bernie (Bernie McCall was our quarterback) to go on a long two. Make sure he lets everyone in the huddle know we are going on two. I don't want anybody jumping offsides," he cautioned as I returned to the field.

These were important instructions since we very seldom went on any other snap count but a quick one. Our offensive philosophy was to sprint to the line of scrimmage, get set and go. Most of the time when we went on a different snap count someone on our offense would move or jump before we got to the unfamiliar starting number.

As I approached the huddle, I could see McCall waving his arms up and down like a duck just learning to fly. The crowd was only about 24,000, so the noise wasn't that loud. Knowing him, I figured he thought it was a cool thing for a quarterback to do.

I got him back towards the huddle and relayed the instructions given to me by the Coach. "Coach wants to run 22 dive," I said. "Now listen, tell everyone that we are going on two. He really wants to be sure that we don't jump offsides. We are going on two, repeat it to everyone."

McCall gave the play to the team in the huddle and then repeated that we were going to try and draw them offsides by going on two. He repeated everything and then finished by saying, "On two, on two."

As we broke the huddle, I lined up at my right guard position and for the first time in the game, OU was in a goal line defense. That meant I was going to go up against Ed McQuarters for the first time. As I got ready to dig in, I noticed how much bigger he looked than his listed 270 pounds. His forearms were huge and he definitely looked determined to prevent us from scoring. I got my 5'11",

220 pound body down in my stance and thought that despite all the threats and warnings from Coach Crowder, there was no way I was going to let this guy kick my ass. At that point, I really didn't know any better.

I got down in my four-point stance, gritted my teeth and got set to make the best block I had ever made. Twenty-two dive was a play that went to our halfback, Billy Symons, right between Jerry McClurg, our right tackle, and me. The beauty of the play was that it was so quick-hitting that the offensive linemen don't have to hold their blocks for very long. All I needed to do was fire out, get my head in the right position, move my feet, and hold my block until the quick Symons could burst through the opening. I was confident that I would out-maneuver McQuarters and show Coach just who was the better man.

McCall got under the center and made his call. I fired out into McQuarters with all the effort and toughness I could muster. I put my face mask right into his chest, slid my head to his outside, grabbed a little of his jersey and started pumping my feet as fast as I could. I could feel some movement and was sure I had gotten him.

But suddenly the bigger and stronger McQuarters positioned his right arm underneath my shoulder pad and flipped me over on my butt. As I looked up, he was staring down at me and said in his Okie accent, "Hey man, you're offsides."

I forgot the snap count. In my determination to show Coach that I wasn't going to let the bigger player get the best of me, I was the one to jump offsides. I remember sheepishly jogging off the field as Coach Crowder screamed, "Get him out of there! Get him off the field!"

*   *   *

Postscript

Ed McQuarters was a very good defensive football player. He played professionally in Canada and was on four Grey Cup teams. He was also inducted into the Canadian Football Hall of Fame.

I learned a good coaching lesson from that experience. Sometimes as coaches, we get our players too fired up. It is vital to ensure that each player is both intense and excited about playing, but misplaced motivation can cost. I was more focused on proving my coach wrong in his estimation of my playing ability, than I was in following the game strategy.

28

Bugs

– Is There an Exterminator in the House? –

A funny thing happened on the way to a game at the University of Oklahoma. I learned that coaches will go to great lengths to guard team secrets.

Coach Eddie Crowder scheduled the team's two-hour, pre-game meeting for 7 p.m. the night before the game. When Coach Crowder said 7, he meant 7! Not 7:15, not 7:10, not even 7:05, but 7 sharp! The meeting was held at our hotel. Crowder had directed the staff to set up the meeting room five chairs short of the expected number of attendees, adhering to the policy of "first come, first served." The last five players to arrive would have to stand for the full two hours. Knowing this, players would try to arrive in plenty of time to get a seat. Sometimes just being on time wasn't enough to guarantee a seat, so many players aimed to get to the meetings 10 to 15 minutes early.

Omitting those five chairs accomplished two things: First, it motivated the players to arrive before the actual meeting time, and second, it gave coaches an easy way to determine who was missing. Dick Mankowski and I were roommates. Both of us were running late in our effort to be "on time." All seats were gone by the time we entered the meeting room at 6:55 p.m. That meant we, along with three other players, would have to stand for the entire two hours. I found a somewhat comfortable place near the door where I could lean against the wall.

The team waited for Coach Crowder to enter the room and start the meeting. These meetings were important. We would review our entire game plan - what plays we were going to run on the goal line, defensive strategies we would use for their third downs plays, etc. This was the coaches' last opportunity to make sure everyone was on the same page for the next day's game.

Coach Crowder entered the room at precisely 7 p.m. He walked directly towards me as I stood against the wall. *Oh, boy, what did I do now?* I thought to myself. But he wasn't interested in me personally; in fact, didn't say even a word to me. Rather, he just motioned for me to move over, away from the room's thermostat that I was standing beside. He then took a small screwdriver out of his shirt pocket and proceeded to unscrew the thermostat. After he inspected the device, he reassembled it, put the screwdriver back in his pocket, and went to the front of the room to start the meeting. Not a word had been spoken. *Weird,* I thought.

* * *

Postscript

Many years later, while I was coaching at the University of Colorado and Crowder was the athletic director, I had a chance to ask him why he checked out hotel thermostats the way he did. He told me that since visiting teams made their hotel reservations far in advance of the game, the home teams could easily find out where they would be staying. He said some coaches would speculate that the visiting team would use one of the hotel's meeting rooms, find out which meeting room it was, and "bug" the room so that they could eavesdrop on the other team's plans. The thermostat was a favorite place to hide the listening device.

I asked Crowder if he thought Coach Bud Wilkinson did that sort of thing. He never answered that question. I assumed from Crowder's non-answer that since he both played for and worked under Coach Wilkinson, the old "bug-in-the-thermostat" routine might have been something he learned during his Sooner days. Did he think Bud would have done that to him?

Section III

Looking Back: The Final Tough Decision

29

Tough, Tougher, Toughest
– Part One –

Every coach has memories of special players - those who stand out both as players and friends long after their playing days are behind them. The longer you coach, the more special memories you have. Pure athletic ability, toughness, grit, discipline, "coachability" and just plain relationships are all considerations when a coach chooses his top players. Not wanting to hurt feelings and recognizing that their lives and careers have been touched by numerous outstanding players over the years, coaches seldom want to publicly name that one "favorite" player.

Being diplomatic yet evasive is usually the easiest way to dodge this recurring question. A coach will frequently say, "I have had so many outstanding players, it is hard to pick one favorite." But way down deep inside we all have that ONE. That one athlete you secretly wished every other player you coached could have been like. That one player who exemplified what you as a coach wanted from all your players.

Ken Marchiol was mine. Yes, over the years I too have had my share of great players who could fill the bill of being my number one. I have been fortunate to have had close and lasting relationships with so many of my former players but Ken exemplified what I wish every player had. A great number of my former players had much of what Ken had. In fact, some were much better at certain things, but none had the total package. Ken had it all.

I had players with better grades but Ken was always a very good student. I never had to worry about him flunking a class or being assigned to the athletic study table.

I had many players who could run faster than Ken but for his size and position he could out-run most. Ken was not the biggest, but at 6'2 1/2" and 245 pounds, he was plenty big enough and excelled at his position of stand-up defensive end.

I coached some VERY TOUGH *hombres* over the course of my career. Ken was as tough as the toughest. On a scale of one to 10, he was an 11. I had a lot of players who were easily 10 and a few who were higher but Ken ranked at the top in the scale of overall toughness.

My first contact with Ken was during his senior year at Trinidad High School in 1983, while I was the head football coach at Mesa State College and in recruiting mode. Ken was not only an outstanding high school football player, but also one of the best wrestlers in the state of Colorado. Ken's father, John, played football with me at the University of Colorado. John was tough as well. He was a running back who had good speed to get to the outside and enough power to run over any opponent. Years later, John had become his son's high school coach. He told me that Ken wanted to wrestle and play football in college. I wasn't that keen on the idea. I believed then and now that while in college, playing football and working towards graduating was overwhelming enough. I told John that if his son came to Mesa State I hoped he would concentrate on football and give up wrestling. He repeated that Ken planned to do both.

Since scholarship monies were limited, I decided to recruit an-

other player, one dedicated solely to football, without the distraction of another sport, and perhaps with equal or maybe even better
football skills than Ken's.

I soon identified another high school player who qualified for a
scholarship and whose skills were quite similar to Ken's. John Garris was from Alamosa High School in Colorado. Ironically, John was
a wrestler as well, but had indicated that he only wanted to play
football in college. Obviously, my type of guy. Like Ken, John was
also a super wrestler and qualified for the state tournament.

Adhering to my strategy, I stalled on my recruiting of Ken and
increased my efforts in trying to convince John to play for Mesa
State College. I told my coaching staff that I thought John was just
as tough as Ken but I was in the minority with this belief. In fact, Bill
Kralicek, my long-time assistant coach, thought I was dead wrong.
Bill had played football and wrestled at the University of Colorado.
He was very good at both. He told me, "You're not even close to be-
ing right on this decision."

It was obvious that I was the only one who thought John was
as tough and therefore as invincible on the field, as Ken. Everyone
agreed that John was tough, but the question persisted as to whether he was tougher than Ken. My pride and unwillingness to share
one of my athletes with another sport, especially one that might encourage him to lose weight, caused somewhat of a riff within my
staff.

Meanwhile, Ken was being aggressively recruited by Adam State
College in Alamosa, Colorado, a school in our conference. When he
learned that I was actively recruiting John Garris for his position, he
signed with Adam State just before wrestling season his senior year.

As fate had it, during the state wrestling tournament Ken and
John both won their first two matches quite easily and were paired
against each other in the 185 pound semi-finals. I planned to at-

tend the highly-touted state match and drove 250 miles through the Rocky Mountains from Grand Junction to Denver, just to see these two warriors battle it out.

The match was scheduled for 6:30 p.m. on a Friday evening and of course I wanted to arrive in plenty of time. As I arrived at the auditorium at about 6:20 p.m., I decided to get a coke and some popcorn before this special fight. After buying my refreshments and while heading towards my seat, I heard the public address announcer introduce both Ken Marchiol and John Garris. The air was electric in anticipation of this highly-touted match. As I settled into my seat a few seconds later, there was a huge roar from the crowd. "What happened?" I asked the coach sitting next to me.

"Ken Marchiol just pinned Garris," he replied.

Looking down to the mat I could see the referee raising Ken's hand in victory. I watched Ken as he calmly walked to the edge of the mat, put his sweat suit on, all the while acting as though nothing extraordinary had just occurred. I watched him as he looked up into the stands and waved to his new head football coach from Adam State College. Ken had pinned his opponent in less than six seconds. The record still stands in Colorado State Wrestling Tournament history.

Apparently, (although I never got to see it) after the referee blew his whistle to start the match, Ken shook John's hand, promptly grabbed him, picked him up and then put him on his back for the three second count by the referee. As simple as that: ONE, TWO, THREE.

I was shocked and upset since I had driven four hours just to watch this match and ONE, TWO, THREE - it was over. It only took six seconds and I didn't see any of it. It happened so fast that my car in the parking lot hadn't even cooled off yet. Of course, being upset at how quickly the match ended was only part of my disappointment. Ken's manhandling of John Garris convinced me that I had recruited the wrong football player.

Ken went on to Adam State and played football, naturally starting his freshman year. John Garris never did enroll at Mesa State. I think he attended the Colorado School of Mines as a wrestler but I am not sure if he ever did play college football.

After his first football season at Adam State, Ken decided he didn't want to wrestle any more. His dad, John, soon called to inquire if Ken could transfer to Mesa State for his second semester.

"Hi Bob. Just wanted to see if you have a need for another linebacker," he began.

Having a good pair of linebackers, I responded, "I am okay there with John Pagano and Daryl McKinnery, but I am looking for a defensive end."

"I think Ken could play that stand-up defensive end for you," his dad stated.

"Actually, I'm looking for a bigger guy to play that position," I responded.

"Ken weighs 220," John replied.

Hmmmmm. *He has really grown from a year ago when he wrestled at 185 pounds,* I thought.

In keeping with athletic protocol, I told John I would have to call Dr. Joel Swisher, the coach at Adam State, to inform him that Ken had inquired about transferring. Following my courtesy call to Coach Swisher, I received a call from Ken himself. "Coach Cortese, I want to come to Mesa State and help you guys win a National Championship in football," he stated.

"What about wrestling?" I asked.

"I'm done with that," he responded. "After getting a taste of college football I have decided to put my time and effort in trying to make it to the NFL. I believe I have a better chance to do that by playing for you guys."

"Not many make it to the NFL," I cautioned.

"I know," he said, "but this is my dream and I think I can do it." So Ken transferred to Mesa State College.

– Part Two –

So how tough was Ken? He was plenty tough. What follows is just one of the incidents I remember about his grit and overall competitiveness.

On December 7, 1985, Mesa State College played in a quarter-final NAIA football championship game. Our opponent was Western Oregon University and we were playing the Wolves at home in Grand Junction, Colorado.

It was a sunny but chilly afternoon and the capacity home crowd was loud. The Wolves were coached by Duke Iverson, a long-time friend and former head coach at Western State College in Gunnison, Colorado. Western State, like Mesa, was in the Rocky Mountain Athletic Conference and was a rival. While Coach Iverson was coaching at WSC we had some intense battles on the football field. He was a good coach who understood the passing game long before it became fashionable to toss the football around.

Ken was playing our right defensive end position. He had made some big plays during the game, but the Wolves were still a powerful offensive team. Their talented quarterback, Tony Burris, was a very smart and accurate passer.

It was a very tight game with the Wolves leading most of the way. In the 4th quarter we finally took the lead 39-32 with 3:43 left in the ball game. After we scored and kicked off, the Wolves took over on their own 32-yard line. They kept us off balance the whole afternoon mostly by passing, but wisely using the running game to keep us honest.

On the third and 10 from their own 32-yard line, Burris dropped back to pass once again. Our game plan was to put pressure on the quarterback in tight situations. We came with an all-out blitz, hoping that we could either hurry Burris into an uncompleted pass or get a sack on him. But by this time their wily old veteran coach, Coach Iverson, had figured out our game plan and called a play we had not seen them run at anytime during our pre-game scouting.

As Burris went back to throw the ball, they released their tight end and flared the running back out into the flat. This enabled Ken to have what we thought was a clear path to sack the unprotected quarterback. WRONG. As Ken was sprinting to make a hit on the seemingly unprotected Burris, their left guard pulled out and caught Ken by surprise. Ken never saw him coming. He was so focused on getting the hit on the quarterback that the guard blasted him with a furious block that knocked him off his feet. BANG. As Ken flew in the air, the talented quarterback dropped a pass to the uncovered running back, who then scooted down the sideline for 50 yards to our 18.

The large home crowd collectively groaned as if the wind had been taken out of their sails. I looked back downfield and saw Ken getting to his knees and holding his left hand as if it were a small canary cradled in his right hand. He was obviously hurt. I had never seen him in such agony.

We took an injury timeout to assess the damage to Ken's hand. Our team doctor, Larry Copeland, and a trainer rushed onto the field to assist Ken. As they helped him off the field, Doc Copeland came to me and said, "Bad news, Coach, Ken has a fractured left hand. He's done for the day. It looks very serious."

I looked at him and asked, "Are you sure, Doc?" (It is amazing some of the dumb things coaches say in the heat of battle. Larry Copeland was one of the best team doctors with whom I had ever been associated, and yet I was questioning his diagnosis.)

"Yup, I am sure," he said. "He's done."

I walked down to Ken and told him he was through for the afternoon. "No way," he shouted back at me. "I can still play. Just move me over to the other side and let me use my right hand. Really, I'll be okay, Coach."

"NO," I said loud and clear. "Take his helmet and hide it from him," I instructed the trainer. I didn't have time to mess with him in this tight situation

With the score still 39–32, I was very anxious to turn my attention to our defense. Our opponents had moved the ball so effectively throughout the game, that I was concerned we couldn't stop them. To add to this stomach-wrenching feeling, I would have to play the remainder of the game without my best pass rusher.

As an added distraction, Ken was becoming a nuisance on the sideline. He was roaming up and down looking for his helmet and cussing out the trainer and Doc Copeland. I finally collared him and told him, "Sit your ass on the bench and shut up." Maybe it was a little stronger than that.

For the next play, the Wolves predictably ran right to where Ken's replacement was playing. BANG – five yards to our 13-yard line. On second down, they ran up the middle and picked up another four yards. It was now third and less than one yard. The clock was running and with less than 30 seconds left in the game they called their second timeout to set up their 3rd down play.

During that timeout Ken was still pissing and moaning about being held out of the game, but the trainers had done a good job of hiding his helmet. Ken wanted to return to the game and was making no secret of it.

As the teams re-entered the field I couldn't help but notice a very confident swagger on the part of the Western Oregon players.

With only two feet to go for the first down with one timeout left and the ball sitting just eight yards from the potential tying score, it was obvious that they liked their chances.

Doc Copeland was standing near me, shaking his head, and yelling something about what a bad idea it was for Ken to be back in the game. I wasn't sure what he meant but as I looked out on the field, Ken was trotting out with the defense. It appeared that he had taken a helmet from one of the freshman players and decided to join his teammates on the field in an attempt to stop the over-confident Wolves. Doc repeated in his best professional bedside manner, "It really is dangerous for Ken to be playing with a fractured hand."

"I know, I know," I shouted back.

I watched as Ken moved over to the other side of the defensive line, trading places with Matt Cunningham, our left defensive end. I assumed he was thinking that by playing the left side, he could protect his bad hand and still be effective using his right hand.

I looked at Ken as our opponents broke the huddle and meandered up to the line of scrimmage. With Doc still blaring in my ear to get Ken off the field, I had to make a quick decision. In the moment of high tension and with the strong urge to stop our opponents from getting the necessary short yardage for a first down, I shrugged my shoulders, acting as if there was nothing I could do at that point. My gut feeling was that an injured Ken playing was still much better than a healthy back-up.

On their third down play the Wolves went back to the swing pass to their running back into the flat - the same play they ran moments earlier for 50 yards. This time they ran it to our left, which was now where Ken was playing. Recognizing the play and knowing that the guard blocked him last time, Ken set his feet and threw a thunderous blow with his right forearm into the pulling guard, knocking him to the ground. He then remembered the quarterback had dropped a pass to the running back, so he raised his left hand high in the air and swatted the pass knocking it to the ground for an incompletion. His left hand was the hand that he fractured earlier. It must have been very painful for him to swat the pass but he did it anyway. Most of us probably would have protected an injured hand and avoided getting it in the path of a flying football passed by a college quarterback. It was obvious that he was in pain from deflecting the pass but as his back-up started onto the field to replace him, Ken waved him off. And I let him.

With the clock stopped and the Wolves needing a first down with one timeout remaining, we weren't sure what play they were going to use. We decided to run our goal line pinch defense and hope that they would try to run a quarterback sneak for the necessary two feet they needed for the first down.

We guessed right and they ran a simple wedge play to their fullback. He took the hand-off and went off-right to the guard, fighting to get the necessary yardage. On this particular defense we had our defensive ends shoot the inside gap. Yep, you guessed it - Ken came slanting down with all the force he could muster with his 240 pounds and hit the ball carrier standing him up, spinning him around and driving him back. No gain, game over. Final score: Mesa State 39, Western Oregon 32.

Postscript

The Western Oregon coaches felt they had gotten a bad spot on the play and went berserk, resulting in three unsportsmanlike conduct penalties in a row.

Ken played the next week with a soft cast on his left hand. Ken Marchiol did make it to the NFL. He played with the New Orleans Saints and the San Francisco 49ers before an injury cut short his pro career. He is now a very successful businessman in Denver where he lives with his wife, Suzy, and three sons - Nicco, Mario, and Santino.

Ken remains committed to athletics and coaches a national youth travel football team. Periodically, he invites me to Denver to help coach his team. I always seem to find time for the old warrior in hopes that we might one day find another young Ken. There aren't many.

Postscript

The definition of the word coach is simply "a person who trains and mentors an athlete or team." I have learned from the best and my life has been personally enriched by countless experiences both on and off the field. I hope my career has lived up to the definition of the word "coach" and that in some small way I might have made a difference in the lives of young athletes. It has been an honor and a privilege to be called *Coach Cortese* for almost four decades.

Every coach has stories similar to those I have shared in this book. Most likely, some are better or more significant than mine. But I would not change anything in my career – it has been a wonderful journey. I have relayed these stories with as much accuracy as possible given the age of my memory and the number of times I have been tackled throughout the years. It was certainly not my intent to hurt or embarrass anyone. I sincerely hope I have not offended anyone or caused any painful memories to resurface. I recognize that I may have embellished some stories or misrepresented some actual conversations. The passage of time has a way of affecting such recollections. In writing this book, my intention was solely to honor the athletes, their families, and the many coaches with whom I have worked. Their presence in my life has made me a better person, and I hope, a better coach.

Coach Bob Cortese
February 2011

Acknowledgments

Writing *Beyond the X's and O's* has been a wonderful experience, providing me the opportunity to revisit almost four decades in the world of coaching. Naturally, all the players, coaches, teammates, friends and family members made these stories possible. In addition, I have benefited from the encouragement and support of many others as I worked to turn this collection of memories into a readable manuscript.

First and foremost, I thank my mentor and good friend, Dr. Jim Alexander, without whom I would never have initiated this journey. Jim facilitated a writers' group which met weekly for over two years in his home. I was honored to participate with Bob Mulcahy, Bob Mullins, Jim Myers and Jay Tompkins as we worked together and critiqued each other's work. These men all contributed to making these stories come back to life. Although Jim did not live to see my work published, his influence and journalistic magic are on every page and I will be forever grateful.

I am also grateful to Jim's wife, Ann, for her kind hospitality and assistance. Putting up with me and the rest of the struggling writers in her home each week was beyond generous.

Thanks also go to my editor, Les Risser, for all the help, encouragement and organization of my thoughts. For a woman who knew very little about football and sports in general, she did a superb job of organizing and refining my thoughts. She was able to capture what I wanted to relate to each of you. This has been a long journey and she and Dr. Alexander taught me so much; they were a godsend.

I owe immense thanks to Lolly Anderson and Ionic Press for holding my hand and walking me through the publishing process after Dr. Alexander passed away. I am also very grateful to her for recommending Les Risser to be my editor.

And special thanks to Hit Design for designing a wonderful cover and for formatting the text.

Finally, I want to thank my wife, Sheila, for her encouragement and constant support in making sure I continued to follow through with this project.

It seems appropriate that once again, I have been part of a team – an incredible team of "players" who made this book a reality.

About the Authors

Coach Bob Cortese

With over 38 years of coaching experience, Bob Cortese has touched the lives of countless student and professional athletes, colleague coaches, and fans. A graduate of the University of Colorado, where he was a member of the Buffalo football team, and the University of Northern Colorado, Coach Cortese has been recognized as "Coach of the Year" 13 times throughout his career. He was inducted into the Mesa State College Hall of Fame in 1995 and the Rocky Mountain Athletic Conference Hall of Fame in 2007. Since retiring from coaching in 2004, he has been active in his community as a sports reporter, newspaper columnist, and Little League umpire. Coach Cortese lives in Edmond, Oklahoma, with his wife, Sheila, and a roomful of trophies.

James E. Alexander, Ph.D.

Dr. James Alexander is the former Dean of the Meinders School of Business at Oklahoma City University. A prolific writer, Dr. Alexander authored or co-authored 26 books, over 1,000 articles, and edited hundreds of books. In addition, he scripted or produced 65 television programs prior to his death in 2010.